MW00657386

The Virginia Creeper Trail Companion

Nature and History along Southwest Virginia's National Recreation Trail

Edward H. Davis
Edward B. Morgan

The Overmountain Press
JOHNSON CITY, TENNESSEE

ISBN 1-57072-065-7
Copyright © 1997 by Edward H. Davis and Edward B. Morgan
All Rights Reserved
Printed in the United States of America

2 3 4 5 6 7 8 9 0

TABLE OF CONTENTS

A steel bridge near Damascus: Horseback riders are common along the Creeper Trail. (Photo by Michael Pierry, Jr.)

PREFACE

The Virginia Creeper Trail, located on thirty-four miles of abandoned railroad right-of-way in Southwest Virginia, was dedicated by Congress as a National Recreation Trail in 1987. One end of the trail is in downtown Abingdon, Virginia, America's first incorporated town west of the Blue Ridge and now ranked as one of America's thirty top small art towns. The other end is just beyond Whitetop Station, which, at 3,576 feet above sea level, was once the highest passenger station east of the Rockies. When the steam engines were running to Whitetop Station just a generation ago, this rail route was considered by railroad buffs to be one of the most scenic in eastern North America.

Although the tracks are gone, the railroad-grade-turned-trail now has more human "traffic" than it had in seventy-seven years of railroad activity: an estimated 25,000 users each year, making it the most traveled trail in Virginia. Damascus, at the trail's midpoint and a major supply point along the Appalachian Trail, was recently designated a "Trail Town USA" by the American Hiking Society, which ranks only the top trail communities in the country. Recent surveys taken along the trail found that people visit this trail for many reasons: bird watching, trout fishing, mountain biking, hiking, horseback riding, wildflower photography, general nature study, and historical appreciation. Some socialize, while others find solitude here.

Already, history, geography, and natural science teachers visit the trail with their students. The landscape is perfect for both formal or informal learning, and many users want to know more about this beautiful corridor. This book attempts an introduction to the abundant history and nature that mingle along this gentle, winding trail.

Our research includes author Ed Morgan's twenty years of fishing and nature observation on the trail, and author Ed Davis's surveys or interviews between 1993 and 1996 with the following people: 120 trail users, thirty adjacent landowners, thirty-five older residents, several local nature and railroad experts, and Joseph A. Rhea, Mrs. George Hall, Martin Hassinger, and Dr. French Moore, Jr., the leader in creating the trail. This was supplemented by Davis's study of aerial photographs and many published and unpublished historical documents, including maps made in 1914 by Virginia-Carolina Railway engineers.

ACKNOWLEDGMENTS

We would like to thank Dr. French Moore, Jr., for his leadership in creating the trail; Jack Barrow, Virginia Department of Transportation, for making available the original railway engineer's maps; Dr. George Treadwell, Professor of Biology at Emory & Henry College, for his help with the tree and wildflower sections; Dr. Doug Ogle, Professor of Biology at Virginia Highlands Community College, for critical comments on the entire manuscript; Jerome Moore for helping with computer software and hardware; and Gary Martel, Director of the Virginia Division of Fisheries for information on fish stocking. Our thanks to the following Emory & Henry College students for geographic research: Alan Aultice, Sharyl Carter, Walter Carter, Todd Creasy, Tabetha Greer, Anna-Maria Hays, Rodney Jessee, John Jones, Jamie King, Jane Duncan Pierce, Tonya Phillips, Gary Puckett, Brian Reed, Shawn Swisher, David Tiller, West Williams, Susan Wood, Chris Workman and Ren Zehmer.

Also we acknowledge the helpful assistance of the members of the Virginia Creeper Trail Club, especially Dr. Mel Heiman, Dr. Bob Horsch, and Tom Horsch; Rev. Frank Honeycutt; author Lloyd D. Lewis; former N & W station agent Mike Hicks; Owen Morgan, Tony Adams, Bill Whitlock, Jim Lovette, and Spike Knuth for input on the geology and natural history sections, and our friends at The Overmountain Press (Archer, Lissa, Sherry, and Bill).

We wish to express our appreciation to Martin Hassinger for permission to use his family's historic photos of the construction of the Creeper Railway and logging in the Mount Rogers region. Special thanks to Jay Baldwin and the Mount Rogers Volunteer Fire Department for assistance with these photographs.

Finally, we would like to thank our partners in life, Sandy Davis and Helen Morgan, for encouraging us along the way.

Whitetop Laurel Creek near Damascus. (Photo by Michael Pierry, Jr.)

INTRODUCTION:
A PLACE TO REVIVE THE SOUL

Geese appear high over us,
pass, and the sky closes. Abandon
as in love or sleep, holds
them to their way, clear,
in the ancient faith: what we need
is here. And we pray, not
for new earth or heaven, but to be
quiet in heart, and in eye
clear. What we need is here.

— from Wendell Berry's "The Wild Geese,"
The Country of Marriage

Our middle daughter, Marta, helped me take an unexpected two-hour sabbath one Wednesday afternoon in the spring. The day before had been an exceptionally long day; I was no good to anybody in town. So we drove down Highway 58, took the back way to Alvarado, parked at the little Bible church there, and started walking west on the Creeper Trail, back towards Abingdon, just daddy and daughter.

The earth was just beginning to wake up as we walked along the Holston River. We listened to the peepers singing their spring song. I spied a groundhog hightailing it into a hole, which led to our subsequent perusal of every hole: "I think there could be a city of gwoun-hogs unnah-neath this duht, Daddy." We wondered about their families and general health. Purple heal-all poked through the soil along the path, thriving alongside a delicate white flower whose name I don't know. The snow had melted and the rains had come. The Holston was a torrent. We were careful not to get too close.

We settled into the riverbank near a calm eddy about a

mile from the car, just before that huge rainbow of a railroad trestle at the confluence of two of the river's forks. We sat on big rocks and threw smaller ones in the water. The middle of the river was full and fast, trashed with all sorts of debris. We spotted large pieces of wood and garbage far upstream, creating a game of pretend and imagination. "I wonder what this might be coming our way?" I'd wonder aloud. And she'd say, "Weelll, Daddy, it might be a shawk." We both decided sharks probably liked salt water for their permanent home, but maybe this one was lost. Our game changed other debris into a boat, a house, a duck. We played for about thirty minutes, a long time for a five year old.

"What are you looking at, Daddy?" She'd caught me staring into the water with that dazed trance found only on the faces of preoccupied adults. While staring I was thinking of lyrics from a famous hymn: "Time like an ever-rolling stream, Soon bears us all away; We fly forgotten as a dream Dies at the op'ning day." Silence. She asked again. "Oh, nothing, honey," I lied. "I'm just thinking."

This trip and many others have made the Virginia Creeper Trail holy ground for me since our move to Abingdon in early 1989. Whether using the trail as a connector to the Mount Rogers Highlands and the Blue Ridge Parkway on spring bicycling trips, or parking at the Watauga Road trailhead for a twice-weekly jog, the Creeper never fails to refresh the spirit and revive the soul. It gives divine perspective in this automated world of schedules, deadlines and ringing telephones. Wendell Berry is right. We pray "to be quiet in heart, and in eye clear. What we need is here."

In the twenty-first chapter of Genesis, the relatively obscure story of Hagar and Ishmael, read closely, is a parable about opening the eyes to grace first missed but always there. It is essentially a story about seeing. Banished into the wilderness by a jealous Sarah, Hagar and his son Ishmael take a bit of bread and a skin of water, wandering until their meager provisions ran out. In desperation, Hagar leaves her child under a bush, unable to watch him die. "What troubles you, Hagar?" God wants to know, apparently unmoved by a dehydrated child and a wildly desperate mother.

Oddly enough in a book bursting with other first-class miracles, there are no such paranormal rescues here. The text casually reports in Genesis 21:19 that "God opened her eyes and she saw a well of water." It does not say that God instantly created that well on the spot, or that the Almighty zapped a little celestial H_2O into her canteen. Instead, Hagar's eyes are opened to a water source that has been there under her nose all along. In her utter hopelessness, she misses it; but God's grace is right there.

One real spiritual life task is simply showing up, being open to God's grace and care wherever we are. What we need is here, but sometimes we need new eyes to see it. Like Lucy and Edmund who walked through an old wardrobe to emerge in C.S. Lewis's wonderfully magical land of Narnia, we too are called to walk through life with our eyes open, ready for the impact when a glance at the familiar suddenly points to the holy, to God. As Elizabeth Barrett Browning wrote in her poem, "Aurora Leigh":

> "Earth's crammed with heaven,
> And every common bush aflame with God.
> But only those who see take off their shoes."

The parables and teachings of Jesus feature many natural objects: seeds, rocks, birds, flowers, streams, trees. Jesus used such familiar sights to direct attention toward the ordinary and on the sacred, revealing truth about the invisible God. Over and over again, Jesus picked up something utterly mundane and said, "The Kingdom of God is like this."

The Virginia Creeper Trail then is a laboratory of the spirit for the hidden Hagar in all God's children. In this era of rugged individualists, we are wooed into believing that we "make it" in this world through self-generated sweat and ingenuity. We foolishly become our own gods, often unaware of our desperate need to connect with the true God. Though linear in direction and precise in termini, the Creeper holds infinite possibilities for grace around every corner, milepost, and trestle. Here on this trail my eyes have been opened on more than one occasion to wells I'd never noticed before, wells offering the gift of refreshment from a source completely outside of self.

Linger. Look. Listen. Drink deeply of the Trail's secrets. What we need is here.

Frank Honeycutt, Pastor
St. John Lutheran Church
Abingdon, Virginia

CHAPTER ONE: NATURE

INTRODUCTION

Nature is now humanized. Go and stand alone in the farthest wilderness and you will eventually see a jet contrail, feel an acid rain, hear a distant truck, or find an old shotgun shell. But we humans are, at the same time, natural. Animal drives lead us to both suffering and enjoyment. We depend on plant and animal ecosystems no less than our ancient predecessors did, and only act (most of the time) like we're not so dependent.

In our wisest moments we appreciate not so much our civilization's climb out of nature but our maturing relationship with it. That relationship has grown through both science and spirituality, in the struggle for both art and livelihood. But for most, livelihood is estranged from nature as we drive, an average of twenty-five minutes to work each morning under glass, work under fluorescent lights, and sleep to the sound of an electric heat pump at night.

What we need is re-creation. That doesn't mean finding absolute wilderness—it no longer exists. Yet, the Virginia Creeper Trail offers miles of relatively natural habitats, as well as time and space for reflection on God's Creation in all its evolving forms. The following sections offer sparks for such reflection. For convenience, the trail is easily divided into two halves: a lower half (Mile 0.0 to Mile 16.0) between Abingdon and Damascus, and an upper half in the higher elevations between Damascus and the trail's end near Whitetop Station (Mile 16.0 to Mile 34.3).

GEOLOGY

Standing on the long curving bridge near the village of Alvarado, where the Creeper Trail crosses the headwaters of South Holston Lake (between Mile Markers 7.0 and 8.0), we

The trail as it crosses the confluence of Middle and South Forks of the Holston River near Mile 8.0. (Photo by Michael Pierry, Jr.)

look northeast in the direction of Damascus to see the confluence of the Middle and South forks of the Holston River. The Middle Fork, approaching on our left, runs muddy, creating a visible demarcation where it joins the clear waters of the South Fork. The two streams seem to run parallel in one channel for a distance, as if reluctant to accept their inevitable integration. Finally they mix to become one river below our feet at the head of South Holston Lake. A river is the essence of the country through which it passes, and the colors of the two streams tell us much about why the Virginia Creeper Railroad was constructed and about the natural wealth that made it possible.

Geographers have divided the contiguous United States into twenty-five provinces based on landforms and geologic history. The boundaries of Virginia contain five of these: the Appalachian Plateau, the Ridge and Valley, the Blue Ridge, the Piedmont, and the Atlantic Coastal Plain. The Virginia Creeper Trail crosses parts of two of these—the Ridge and

Valley and the Blue Ridge—with Damascus as both the trail's midpoint and the gateway between the two provinces.

The Ridge and Valley Province, sometimes referred to as the Great Valley of Virginia, is characterized by sedimentary rocks—primarily limestones, dolomites, sandstones, and shales. It consists of relatively flat or rolling valleys divided by parallel ridges. The limestone was created from the skeletons and shells of sea animals that lived in the ocean covering this region millions of years ago. The dolomites, shales, and sandstones were formed from layers of sediments also deposited in that long-departed sea. Over millions of years, collisions between parts of the earth's crust caused these thick rock layers to bend and fold. Since then erosion by water and wind has removed much of the original rock—especially the limestone, dolomites, and shales—while sandstones have been more resistant. These harder rocks have, in fact, protected the weaker rocks beneath them, leaving the ridges that run mostly southwest to northeast through the province.

Millions of years of weathering created the long parallel valleys and the deep limestone soils that make this province well-suited for both agriculture and transportation. Attractive to early settlers, the region was eventually an important historic and modern pathway through Appalachia.

To the south and east of the Ridge and Valley Province lies the Blue Ridge Province. This province is composed of igneous and metamorphic rock formed when the Appalachian Mountains were thrust upward in an even earlier period than the one mentioned above. Today's Blue Ridge Mountains are worn and rounded, but their original peaks were at least four miles high, rivaling the Himalayas in Asia.

Yet the Blue Ridge Province boasts superlatives even today: Virginia's two highest mountains, Mount Rogers and Whitetop Mountain (respectively 5,729 and 5,520 feet) near the Virginia Creeper Trail. Both mountains are composed of volcanic rock, and, like much of the Blue Ridge, are rough and rocky, with soils unsuited for agriculture. Since travel in the province could be difficult, early settlers largely bypassed this region in favor of the better soils in the Ridge and Valley Province.

The contrasting character of these two provinces is best told by the rivers that drain them. The Middle Fork of the Holston passes through the Ridge and Valley's agricultural lands, picking up tons of silt that color it a distinct chocolate brown even in drought. The Holston River's South Fork drains a heavily forested watershed in the mostly undeveloped Blue Ridge Province, so it passes under the Creeper Trail mostly clean and clear.

Traveling the Virginia Creeper's thirty-four miles gives a firsthand view of unique geomorphology—or lay of the land—of these regions. The land's character is ultimately shaped by rain, rivers, and the chemical and physical properties of the rocks beneath. Different landforms have long been recognized as appropriate for particular land uses: level to rolling land for crops, hilly or rocky land for pasture, and steep or very rocky land for forests. Where land managers respect these differences, stream quality is usually preserved. Soil erosion above the Middle Fork of the Holston, however, results largely from lack of buffer land between pasture, crops, and river.

The trailhead in Abingdon is well within the Ridge and Valley Province, with its accordion-folded and faulted rocks. In addition to the folds there, geologists have identified many faults (thankfully inactive) or giant cracks in the earth's crust. Millions of years ago, earthquakes were common here as crustal pieces scraped and shifted against each other along these faults. One ancient fault, called the Spurgeon Fault, runs almost directly underneath the trailhead at Green Springs Road. The trail crosses several others, including the Alvarado and Damascus faults.

The most prominent rocks seen along this section of the trail are the dark blue-grey limestone and dolomite outcrops. Part of the Conococheague, Honaker, and Chepultepec formations from the early Paleozoic era, they are about 500 million years old. Outcroppings near the golf course (between Mile Markers 1.0 and 2.0) are Chepultepec limestone.

Geologists study exposed surfaces of folded and faulted

Soil Erosion along the Middle Fork

Although a natural difference marks the waters of the two rivers due to the rocks and soil through which they drain, land use practices make Middle Fork waters dirtier now than in the past. Public awareness of poor water quality grew in the early 1980s when Marion residents noticed an odor from their drinking water. Soon their grass roots movement to address the problem was joined by the Tennessee Valley Authority, the Soil Conservation Service (now the Natural Resource Conservation Service), and the New River Highlands Resource Conservation and Development Council. Representatives from these federal agencies met with local residents to create the Middle Fork Holston Water Quality Committee.

Since then, water quality has improved through a variety of efforts. Local farmers built fences to keep cattle off stream banks and out of streams. Runoff from large livestock operations has been reduced. An example of these "best management practices" (BMPs) is Dave Johnson's dairy farm near Glade Spring. Although his cows graze quite close to the Middle Fork, Johnson reduced manure runoff to nearly zero through fencing and manure recycling. As more BMPs are adopted, Middle Fork waters should begin to clear; but, for now, TVA studies estimate that some fields in the watershed are eroding at a rate of more than 100 tons of soil per acre yearly. To find out more, see Chapter Four: Resources.

rocks to determine underlying geological structures. For example, local geologist Dr. Charles Bartlett's study of an exposed Chepultepec limestone formation just a few miles east of the trail determined its thickness there to be 855 feet. Such depth of deposit gives one an appreciation for the millions of years required to create them on the ancient ocean floor.

Just past the golf course, the trail passes through two low ridges, the Great Knobs and the River Knobs. While the Great Knobs may not seem that "great" relative to the nearby mountains, these ridges indicate a difference in rock formation. There is a reason those hills are there!

The Great Knobs and River Knobs represent in miniature the process that created the Ridge and Valley Province. The knobs are remnants of synclines (inverted arches of rock) that have severely eroded. They are part of the Athens formation of siltstone and shale layers that are more resistant to rainfall, streams, and groundwater than the surrounding limestone. Dr. Bartlett estimates the Athens formation thickness at about 1,000 feet in the Great Knobs, though they rise only about 240 feet above the valley where the trail runs. Saw-edged fossils of the graptolite, a tiny ancient animal, are found in the Athens shale along the trail.

Traveling between the Great Knobs and the River Knobs southeast, the trail winds around the Watauga community and crosses the Watauga anticline, an eroded arch of limestone rock. Here limestone layers mix with layers of chert—or flint—hard, glass-like rock once used by Native Americans to make tools and arrowheads. These limestones, called the Knox group, have been eroded down to a relatively flat valley floor, with Fifteenmile Creek and underground streams carrying the weathered rock slowly toward the Holston River.

As the trail approaches South Holston Lake (near Mile Marker 7.0), it crosses the Conococheague formation, consisting of blue and dark grey limestone mixed with layers of chert. Portions have eroded into Karst topography, a type of land form named for a region in Yugoslavia noted for sinkholes, caves, and springs. Several small sinkholes can be seen along the trail, indicating underground chemical erosion of limestone. These may be considered tips of geological icebergs. Much larger holes may be found underneath such a landscape.

Along the shores of South Holston Lake, about a mile from the trail's large curving trestle, is the site of a nineteenth century iron mine. Although Virginia once had several such commercial mining districts—iron production ranked fourth in the nation in 1900—iron was never a major economic resource here. The presence of the valuable ore sparked

Rock cliffs are adjacent to the trail in nearly all sections. This is Whitetop Laurel Creek at about Mile 22.0. (Photo by Edward H. Davis.)

Damascus's development in the late 1800s, and nearby Laurel Bloomery, Tennessee, was the home of a simple iron refinery (then called a bloomery). However, the development of Minnesota's Mesabi iron deposits made local iron production uncompetitive.

Just south of the Middle and South Forks junction, one can see old terrace deposits along the stream banks, indicating that the South Fork of the Holston River once flowed at a much higher elevation, having cut through to its present bed. These terraces consist of unconsolidated silt, sand, and clay with an intermixture of gravel and small boulders called cobbles.

These cobbles are more readily seen where they have been used in building many homes, fences, and outbuildings in Damascus. The trail passes numerous "riverstone" buildings, including the beautiful Rock School. Built during the Great Depression as a public works project, the school contains thousands of cobbles gathered from the stream channel during periods of low flow. Miles of rolling in fast waters were required to produce the cobbles' smooth surfaces and rounded shapes.

Cobblestones introduce the trail user to the Blue Ridge Province. The fast-running tributaries of the Holston's South

Whitetop Mountain is often snow covered in the winter months. (Photo by Edward H. Davis)

Whitetop Mountain

Made of fine-grained igneous rock (mostly rhyolite), Whitetop Mountain stands at 5,520 feet, Virginia's second highest mountain *mass*. (The second highest mountain *peak* in Virginia is actually the little-known Balsam Mountain, an outlier—or shoulder—one-half mile east of the Mount Rogers peak.) According to nationally noted naturalist Dr. Douglas Ogle, the name *Whitetop* was not the mountain's first. Early maps show it as *Meadow Mountain*, but in a 1772 treaty with the Cherokee Indians, *Whitetop Mountain* is used. Both Whitetop and Meadow refer to the light-colored field which stands in sharp contrast to the dark red spruce growing on part of the mountain's crest. The name *Whitetop* may also originate from snow on that meadow throughout much of winter, while the lower lands from which it is viewed (and named) are less often snow covered.

Today, the U.S. Forest Service owns most of Whitetop Mountain's upper elevations, but the mountain is surrounded by the old communities of Konnarock on the north, Green Cove on the west, and Whitetop Station on the south. When trains were running, Whitetop Station, at an elevation of 3,576 feet, was the highest point for passenger train service in the eastern United States. East of Whitetop is a high gap called Elk Garden, and then Mount Rogers, Virginia's highest mountain at elevation 5,729 feet—only 209 feet taller than Whitetop.

Adventurous hikers may detour from the Creeper Trail to visit Whitetop Mountain via the Appalachian Trail (A.T.). At the Creek Junction trestle's southern (uphill) end, about Mile 27.3, you'll see the A.T. leave the Creeper Trail heading east. From there you'll climb over Lost Mountain and cross U.S. 58 and Va. 601 before climbing toward the top of Whitetop Mountain. A side trail from the A.T. makes the final ascent. The hiking distance from the Creeper Trail to the top of Whitetop is about eight miles. This is a difficult trip, so be prepared. Please note that bikes are not allowed on this trail. Another way to climb to the top of Whitetop is by car, taking the gravel Forest Service road from Elk Garden on the mountain's east side.

Fork must have provided considerable power to carry and shape such large cobbles. This province provides sandstone and quartzite bedrock from which the stones are slowly carved.

Approaching Damascus, one sees the landscape change. Now tall ridges jut up from the valley floor, again evidence of the Blue Ridge Province. These sandstone rocks at the base of the Iron and Holston mountains are much harder than the nearby limestone and shale. The ridges, part of the Chilhowie formation, were thrust up and over a granite "basement," which gives this part of the Blue Ridge its prominent height.

The trail continues across the Chilhowie group almost until Creek Junction (about Mile 26.0). Here the sandstones abut against glacial deposits of the Konnarock Formation. Left behind by a very ancient ice age, not the last ice age which ended about 10,000 years ago, these glacial deposits can be recognized in the "conglomerates" found in large boulders and rock cliffs next to the trail.

Near Green Cove (about Mile 30.0), the geology shows an unusual twist as the trail crosses the Mount Rogers Formation. Not readily apparent from the surface, underlying rocks here are composed of ancient lavas, rubble, and ash deposited by volcanic activity about 750 million years ago. The geology of Mount Rogers was not understood until the 1970s since previous field work failed to recognize either volcanic or glacial processes. Today, geologists understand that both Mount Rogers and Whitetop Mountain were part of a large volcano, called the Mount Rogers volcanic center. Now, with the frightening force of the earth's interior heat applied elsewhere, we should not fear new eruptions here.

From the Creeper Trail's beginning in Abingdon to its end near Whitetop at the North Carolina border, one travels over some of the most varied geology in the eastern United States. Few regions offer such variety over such a short distance: sinkholes and caves, ancient volcanoes, and glacial deposits. When you stop along the trail to remove a troublesome stone from your boot, consider the rock's origin: it might have been part of a volcano!

The Naming of Mount Rogers

First called Balsam Mountain, after the trees (firs or "balsams") that grow there, the highest point in Virginia was renamed Mount Rogers by the Virginia Legislature in the 1800s to honor William Barton Rogers. An educator and scientist, Rogers initiated the first comprehensive study of Virginia's geology.

Born in Philadelphia in 1804, Rogers had a distinguished career at William and Mary College and the University of Virginia. He was appointed the commonwealth's first state geologist in 1835 and began Virginia's first geological survey. At the time, geology was a new field, and little was known about Virginia's geology.

Unfortunately, funding was dropped in 1842, and Rogers moved to Boston, where he founded the Massachusetts Institute of Technology (M.I.T.) in 1862.

FORESTS

The Creeper Trail is a narrow ribbon laid through forest, field, and town. Trail users and mowing machines keep about fifteen to twenty-five feet cleared, but the right-of-way averages fifty feet wide. Outside of townscapes and some farms, the trail and right-of-way lands comprise a corridor of forest with a total area of more than 300 acres. Perhaps ten percent of the trail's length is under closed canopy, as original trees or fast-growing new ones prosper adjacent to the trail. This corridor has gradually become home to many non-native trees and shrubs. (One example is the tree-of-heaven, *Ailanthus altissima*, spreading along one side of the trail at Mile 27.0 in Creek Junction. This species was imported from China long ago as an ornamental.) Numerous planted trees can be seen between the trailhead in Abingdon and Mile 2.0, and rose bushes (non-native) are found at various sites near farmsteads.

Old trees can be found, but "old growth forest" does not exist along the trail. In the lower section (Mile 0.0 to Mile 17.0), farmers and Native Americans before them cleared the land for crops and grazing. An old Indian village was excavated just downstream from the confluence of the Middle and South Forks of the Holston (Mile 8.0). On the upper section (Mile 17.0 to Mile 34.0), the lumber companies cut valuable trees close to the transportation system built to export their product.

To identify particular old age stands, look for trees of great breadth or height, with a large number of standing dead trees, fallen logs, and a pit-and-mound pattern on the forest floor. (The pit-and-mound topography is created when trees are uprooted during high winds and ice storms.) Also, expect older forest on the sunny and dry south-facing slopes to be shorter and more open. Wet, shady coves have a closed canopy and larger trees, but these trees may be younger than the shorter ones on the dry sites. The largest stand of mature forest is between Taylor's Valley and Creek Junction (Mile 24.0 to 26.8), much of it on the north-facing slope of Chest-

Red Oak log cut near Konnarock, circa 1910, using special 10-ft. crosscut saw—the typical saw was 5 or 6 feet long. (Photo courtesy of Martin Hassinger.)

nut Mountain along Whitetop Laurel Creek.

Inadvertent landscaping resulted from the railroad years. Apple cores and seeds tossed from trains created the lush crop of apples along the trail today. However, wheel and locomotive sparks and tossed cigarettes caused brush fires and cut short the recovery of native forest flowers and trees, limiting and rearranging the diversity of species. Perhaps the most dangerous threat today is kudzu. Imported sixty years ago to reduce erosion along highways, this is now a serious threat to native plant communities throughout the South. The largest kudzu colonies along the trail are found alongside U.S. Highway 58, especially around Miles 20.0 and 21.0, uphill from Damascus.

Hoping to reduce the threat of fire, railroad companies had policies of intense right-of-way management. Grasses and wildflowers were kept away from the tracks with herbicides, and trees and branches were manually cut back. Since 1977, when the railroad was abandoned, grasses have recovered some of the raised railroad bed. Mowing machines, however, prevent most wildflowers and new tree seedlings from growing close to the trail. Still, in the long run, closed canopy may result if trees already established are allowed to grow and spread their branches overhead. Long sections crossing farmland provide a little contrast. Like most of the steeper Appalachians, this area is appearing more and more like it must have before 1900, when forests on the upper section were mature and rich in diversity. Indeed, some biologists argue that the deeper coves of the Southern Appalachians are the most diverse temperate forests in the world, with more than 100 types of trees and more than 1,300 flowering plant species. Don't expect that diversity along the trail, however. Many plant species that were lost from this region during the cutting and burning of the 1910s and 1920s have never returned because their habitat was destroyed.

Now that the forests have recovered from turn-of-the-century burning and cutting, logging is once again practiced in private and public forest lands near the Creeper Trail. More than half of the land in the Mount Rogers National

Recreation Area is designated for timber cutting under commercial contracts. However, less than one percent of the land in the Jefferson National Forest is logged in any given year, and less than ten percent of that logging is clear-cutting. Little or none of the logging is visible from the sixteen miles of trail through that national forest. The Recreation Area also contains several designated wilderness areas, none of them along the trail. In fact, because the region's tourism income ($379 million annually for Southern Appalachia) is much larger than timber's ($32 million), the current trend is toward less logging on public land.

Some trees along the trail are very large, the best known being the massive white oak just off the right-of-way about 100 yards from the trailhead in Abingdon. Other very large trees may be found, especially along the upper section of the trail. These oldest trees are mostly oaks, yellow poplar, and eastern hemlock. Some uncommon trees that are known to grow locally, but which the authors have not yet seen, are the balsam poplar, the roundleaf birch, and the dotted hawthorn.

A 1994 tree survey indicates the most dominant trees along the trail are white pine, black cherry, black locust, yellow birch, red maple, eastern hemlock, eastern redcedar and yellow poplar. Since nearly all of the trail is within narrow valleys near streams rather than on ridges, the vegetation naturally reflects moderately moist conditions. However, the list of trees also reflects the human impact of logging, forest fires, clearing for buildings, and railroad maintenance (1880-1976). Today's forest is not a "natural" forest since the original forest was dominated by a different set of trees. According to a recent survey done in a mature stand in the Jefferson National Forest, dominant trees along the trail's mountainous stretches before the twentieth century probably included northern red oak, sugar maple, chestnut oak, scarlet oak, basswood, Fraser magnolia, American beech, eastern hemlock and white pine.

Older residents here would point out a major absence from both lists: the American chestnut. One of the most

Will Hassinger (right) stands by a mature white pine tree. (Photo courtesy of Martin Hassinger.)

important species in southern Appalachian forests was the American chestnut, constituting a third of all trees in some forests until a blight hit between about 1904 and 1940. Although millions of sprouts still exist in Washington County, especially in high coves and on sandy ridges where the hiker may find a small American chestnut tree along the trail, these are doomed to catch the blight. Even blighted trees in good sunny locations grow up to five feet in height per year; but the disease prospers as well, killing the trees in about ten years. Trees in shady sites grow very slowly, reaching not more than twenty feet in height and surviving as many as forty years since the disease does not spread as quickly in such conditions.

Fred Hebard, plant pathologist with the American Chestnut Foundation's Meadowview (Virginia) Research Farm, says some American chestnut trees in this county are fifty feet in height and twenty inches in diameter at breast height. Research is under way locally to breed a resistant American chestnut by cross-hybridization with the Chinese chestnut. In about ten years, the Meadowview Research Farm plans to provide the public with blight-resistant American chestnuts, perhaps making it possible for forest canopies to once again include these giants.

Meanwhile, many local residents planted Chinese chestnut trees as ornamentals during the decline of the American variety. These now mature beautiful trees, producing large crops of chestnuts, are reminders of the prominence of chestnuts in southern Appalachian culture in the 1800s. You might see old fences made of split chestnut logs since fencing was a major use for chestnut. One other monument to the chestnut tree is Chestnut Mountain. Two miles due east of Taylors Valley, Chestnut Mountain's peak is at 4,040 feet elevation. This mountain is best viewed on the trail around Mile 29.0 between Taylors Valley and Green Cove.

The Christmas Tree Industry

Creeper Trail travelers pass several Christmas tree plantations, usually consisting of rows of Fraser fir. This industry was nonexistent when logging first began in this region. Today, the 15,000 growers in the U.S. produce one billion dollars in sales each year. Nationwide, about 35 million trees are harvested yearly with the Upper Midwest holding the majority of these farms. However, landowners and investors in many rural counties of Appalachia have turned to this crop since the 1970s. The crest of Whitetop Mountain provides views of dozens of such tree farms scattered across the mountainsides. Currently, small- and medium-sized farms can be seen near the Creeper Trail, but someday they may compete in size with those of the Midwest.

Christmas tree farming began in the Whitetop, Virginia, area in the late 1970s when the Fraser fir was identified as a tree which could be grown successfully in this region. Fraser firs, described by foresters as the "Cadillac of the Christmas tree industry," are perhaps the ideal Christmas tree. They have a deep rich green foliage, and their branches are strong and support heavy ornaments without sagging. Fraser firs have an excellent aroma and hold their needles well, even in overheated homes. These trees occur naturally only on Mount Rogers in Virginia and in extremely limited high elevation areas of North Carolina and Tennessee. They normally grow well only in elevations above 3000 feet. The trees grow slowly and can take up to twelve years to be large enough to qualify as a first-rate Christmas tree. The Fraser fir groves on Mount Rogers and in other regions have been injured by the balsam wooly aphid, a tree killing insect that was accidentally imported from Asia.

Prior to the inception of the Christmas tree industry, farmland in the Mount Rogers and Whitetop area was used primarily for livestock grazing and some tobacco production. Fraser fir Christmas tree farming has proven to be the ideal agricultural crop for this community and has helped to keep the land in production rather than second-home development.

The nation's largest grower, The Kirk Company based in Wisconsin, typically produces 400,000 trees per year, both Scotch pine and Fraser fir, on one of its many farms. The Kirk Company promotes the industry as environmentally positive since it retains forest cover on marginal land and uses dead trees by grinding them into mulch or by enhancing fish habitat in lakes. Opponents argue that tree farms are too sterile to serve as replacements for natural forests, and pesticides used on the trees might damage both natural systems and human water supplies. For now, this debate is far from resolved.

Most of Whitetop Mountain's old growth forest passed through this millpond between 1906 and 1928 on its way to the saw blade, the flatbed railcar, and points far beyond the reach of the Virginia Creeper Railway. (Photo courtesy of Martin Hassinger.)

Look for Christmas tree plantations near Green Cove and Whitetop Station, between Mile 29.0 and Mile 34.0. Please do not leave the trail to walk among these trees, however, since they are on private land.

Tree Species

A great diversity of tree species can be seen along the trail's thirty-four miles. Dr. George Treadwell and Dr. Edward H. Davis of Emory & Henry College have identified the following sixty species along the trail:

- ☐ apple
- ☐ ash, green
- ☐ ash, white
- ☐ basswood
- ☐ beech, American
- ☐ birch, sweet
- ☐ birch, yellow
- ☐ buckeye, yellow
- ☐ cherry, black
- ☐ cherry, fire
- ☐ cottonwood, eastern
- ☐ cucumbertree
- ☐ dogwood, alternate-leaf
- ☐ dogwood, flowering
- ☐ fir, Fraser
- ☐ hackberry
- ☐ hemlock, eastern
- ☐ hickory, pignut
- ☐ hickory, shagbark
- ☐ hornbeam
- ☐ horse-chestnut
- ☐ locust, black
- ☐ magnolia, fraser
- ☐ magnolia, bigleaf
- ☐ maple, silver
- ☐ maple, ashleaf
- ☐ maple, striped
- ☐ maple, sugar
- ☐ maple, red
- ☐ mountain laurel
- ☐ mountain winterberry
- ☐ mulberry, red
- ☐ oak, white
- ☐ oak, chestnut
- ☐ oak, northern red
- ☐ oak, black
- ☐ oak, blackjack
- ☐ oak, pin
- ☐ oak, scarlet
- ☐ osage-orange
- ☐ pine, Scotch
- ☐ pine, white
- ☐ pine, Virginia
- ☐ redbud
- ☐ redcedar, eastern
- ☐ rhododendron, rosebay
- ☐ Russian-olive
- ☐ sassafras
- ☐ serviceberry
- ☐ sourgum
- ☐ sourwood
- ☐ sumac, winged
- ☐ sumac, staghorn
- ☐ sycamore
- ☐ tree-of-heaven
- ☐ tuliptree
- ☐ walnut, black
- ☐ white-cedar, northern
- ☐ willow, black
- ☐ witch-hazel

Common Trees of the Lower Section

Flowering dogwood (*Cornus florida*—Virginia's state tree) was once a key resource for the textile industry. Throughout the South, dogwood trees were cut in large numbers to make shuttles for mechanical looms here and around the world. No other wood was so strong and smooth. The best dogwood logs were found in old-growth forest, where trunks grew relatively tall and straight. By the 1930s and 1940s dogwoods had become somewhat endangered from harvests in excess of growth. Today, with looms using plastic shuttles, dogwoods are again plentiful and show wondrous blossoms along the trail in May. Unfortunately, a disease called dogwood anthracnose, accidentally introduced from overseas, is killing dogwoods at a high rate, especially in cool, wet habitats such as the high coves and dark forests of Appalachia. Another element of traditional beauty in our region may disappear.

Black cherry *(Prunus serotina*—also called wild cherry) is famous for its beauty in furniture. The old-growth forests required for large, straight, and knotless cherry trees are essentially gone. Cherry trees indicate the sites of old fences all along the trail, since birds ate the fruit and deposited the seeds where they perched along these fences of old. Some sections of the trail between Abingdon and Damascus show forests with cherry trees in the majority of trees. At the trail's higher elevations (Mile 30.2 and Mile 31.0) you will see fire cherry trees, a less common species with small, bright red fruit from July to September.

Sassafras *(Sassafras albidum)* was once very popular as a source of tea, which is made by boiling well-washed sassafras roots until the water turns brownish-red, then sweetening to taste. This rather small tree is found in many places along the trail, but don't expect to make your tea here: digging up trees is not allowed! Leave the tree to provide fruit each autumn for birds and squirrels and to provide twigs each winter for deer.

Black locust *(Robinia pseudoacacia)* trees, once found only in Southern Appalachia, are now spread throughout the USA and Europe. The reason: human intervention, coupled with the tree's unexcelled strength, durability, and fuelwood value. Locust makes excellent fence posts on farms. Virginia's Native Americans made locust bows. Local people once made fritters with the locust's fragrant white flowers. One recipe: Pick the flower clusters in the morning when they are freshest. Heat one-inch-deep oil in a frying pan. Mix a batter of eggs and flour. Coat the flower clusters and fry until crisp. Locust blossoms are found all along the trail, especially in sunny locations, in April, May, and June.

Eastern redcedar *(Juniperus virginiana*—also called Virginia juniper) grows along the trail in sunny locations, especially along fence lines where birds often deposit seeds. Birds of many kinds eat the fruit of this tree, thus insuring widespread distribution. People first settling this region used redcedar for fences, shingles, and coffins because it resists weathering so well. The greatest demand, however, was for use in pencils, due to its lightness and ease in sharpening. Prices for cedar wood were so high in the 1910s that many old cedar fences and shingles were taken from this region to be manufactured elsewhere as pencils!

Staghorn sumac *(Rhus typhina*—also called shumake), considered a weed by most locals, is a very popular ornamental in Europe. This plant has played many roles in addition to providing bright autumn colors. In Southwest Virginia, people would cut sumac twigs and leaves to sell to nearby tanneries, which used the extract to cure the best leathers. The name, in fact, may derive from that use, since it was used by shoemakers! Another use of the hairy fruit is to make a cool drink, sour like lemonade: Between June and September pick the upright red fruit cluster, rub the fruit to bruise slightly, soak in very cold water for fifteen minutes, strain the result through cheesecloth to remove hairs and large pulp, and sweeten to taste. Native Americans taught early settlers to make this drink. The plant called **poison sumac** *(Rhus vernix)* is indeed poisonous, but not easily confused with true sumac: poison sumac berries are whitish in drooping clusters and are uncommon in this area.

Sycamore (*Platanus occidentalis*—some call it planetree, others Virginia maple) is recognized by its peeling white bark and large, bright green leaves. The sycamore's location can be predicted better than any other tree on the trail: it cannot prosper in higher elevations, and it likes streams. Seeds are designed to tolerate watery sojourns and winters in the mud. Eventually, such a seed can produce the largest tree (in diameter) in Eastern North America. Giant sycamores were cut long ago for lumber, despite their low quality. However, hollow sycamore trunks were used to house pioneers while they built cabins along rivers.

Common Trees of the Upper Section

Rhododendron *(Rhododendron maximum*—called laurel by many) is a proud symbol of Appalachia. Easily confused with mountain laurel, which has similar but smaller leaves, rhododendron is seen along higher trail elevations and is healthiest in shaded coves. Rosebay rhododendron has white or pink blossoms. Elsewhere in our region are the purple flowers of Catawba rhododendron. Rhododendron thickets were classic hideaways for illegal alcoholic beverage manufacture (moonshining, that is). Creeper Trail users have yet to see a still, and maybe that's due to the density of the thickets. To enjoy the beautiful blossoms, travel the trail in May and June.

Eastern hemlock *(Tsuga canadensis)* dominates the landscape on the trail's upper section. Green Cove Creek, for example, flows under hundreds of large hemlocks, washing the roots of the trees. Local trout feed daily on insects dropping from hemlock branches, and a carpet of brown hemlock needles harbors many chipmunks and other small animals on the shaded forest floor. Unrelated to the poisonous hemlock which Socrates drank, this tree could save your life. The inner bark holds many concentrated nutrients, waiting to serve a person lost and hungry. Even Vitamin C is obtainable: just brew a tea with the light green younger needles. Earlier residents even made brooms from the branches.

Sugar maple *(Acer saccharum)* is common enough that nearly every local resident recognizes it. Few area people, however, have witnessed the sugar-making process discovered by Native Americans. Travelers on the Creeper Trail's higher elevations are looking at forests that were part of a major maple syrup industry in the nineteenth century. After 1910 the short-term lumber value of maple trees was given precedence over syrup industry needs. Today only a few maple syrup producers remain, but each year the volunteer fire department on Whitetop holds a maple syrup festival. When sugar maple is allowed to grow old in a forest, its sapwood is called hard maple and is considered great wood for flooring.

Red maple *(Acer rubrum)* is perhaps the most widespread tree in Eastern North America. Growing almost anywhere, red maple is a popular ornamental tree and one of the dominant trees along the trail. Red maple prospers best in moist, cool, shady spots, so look there for larger specimens. The best time of year for viewing the red maple is fall, when it becomes the main reason the trail sides are red.

Tuliptree *(Liriodendron tulipifera*—also called yellow poplar, popple, and canoewood) is the tallest hardwood tree on this continent—if allowed to grow old. Indeed it never looks "old," since its trunk is typically clean and ramrod straight. A fast-growing tree, tuliptree is planted for its timber, which is light and easily worked. Unfortunately, few tuliptrees reach maturity since the wood is used to make paper. Along the trail, large specimens can be seen between Mile Markers 21.0 and 22.0 (just downhill from Taylors Valley).

Shagbark hickory *(Carya ovata)* sustained generations of our ancestors. Young people once gathered at "nut cracks" to socialize and stuff their stomachs with hickory nuts. Prior to this, Native Americans depended on the sweet cooking oil extracted from hickory nuts. Today, the wood is better known than the nut, since hickory smoke is what gives the best barbecue its flavor. Hams have traditionally been smoked with green hickory fires, and hickory has always been a favorite fuelwood. A large old hickory can be seen at Mile 18.2, uphill from Damascus, and another at Mile 23.0 in Taylors Valley.

Cucumber tree *(Magnolia acuminata)* is found along the higher, more shady reaches of the trail. It has large elliptical leaves and dark red cone-shaped fruit. These cones were used long ago to treat fever as an infusion in whiskey. Its unusual character has led to its planting as an ornamental throughout the eastern states.

VIRGINIA CREEPER VINE

(Parthenocissus quinquefolia)

In virtually every forested section of the trail one can see the Virginia creeper vine, for which the railway was originally named. A common woody vine of the Southern Appalachian Mountains—though probably less common before the railroad's construction—this plant loves the partial sunlight maintained along the railroad/trail corridor since about 1900. One reason the plant is well established is that its seeds are hidden in a fruit with high fat content. Many birds and mammals use these deep blue fruits to fatten themselves for winter. Dispersal of seeds follows as they pass through their carrier unharmed. One can recognize the Virginia creeper vine by its compound leaf which has five leaflets extending like fingers.

In autumn the leaves turn orange-red. Be careful when observing this vine, as it often grows intermixed with poison ivy.

WILDFLOWERS

Timing is everything is a common saying that applies well to comedy and wildflowers alike. Many of the best-loved wildflowers have unpredictable bloom periods of one month or less. As weather varies, spring and fall are periods whose coming and going will vary by weeks from year to year. Also, elevation affects climate on a very local scale: plants blooming in Abingdon during April can be revisited in May at Green Cove! So if you want to see wildflowers on the Creeper Trail, remember that the more you use the trail, the greater are your chances for a find. To really appreciate these small plants, it is advisable to carry a magnifying glass to open up a world of bizarre shapes and subtle hues.

Following is a list of twenty-two wildflowers known to bloom along the right-of-way, and the approximate bloom dates. If you are ambitious, wander to the edge of the right-of-way in early spring to seek out numerous species not listed here. Good guidebooks are listed in the bibliography.

Common Name	Season	Flower Appearance	Size	Where to Look
bellwort	Apr-May	yellow drooping	1"	anywhere
bloodroot	Apr-May	white, gold center	1"	stream banks
blue violet	May-Jun	4 blue petals	⅔"	shady areas
buttercup	Mar-Jun	shiny yellow cup	1"	anywhere
columbine (wild)	May-Jul	5 scarlet petals	2"	rocky areas
dandelion	Feb-Jun	yellow sunburst	1"	sunny areas
dwarf iris	Apr-May	violet/white	2"	lower elev.
fire pink	May-Jun	crimson star	1"	dry areas
foamflower	Apr-Jun	long white cluster	3"	high forests
heal-all	Apr-Oct	dense purple spike	½"	anywhere
ironweed (purple)	Aug-Sep	purple clusters	3"	damp areas
joe-pye weed	Aug-Sep	large pink cluster	5"	anywhere
mayapple	Mar-Apr	waxy white	2"	shady areas
pipsissewa	Jun-Jul	small nodding white	⅔"	dry woods
Solomon's seal	Apr-May	tiny white bells	⅔"	lower elev.
spring beauty	Mar-Apr	white/pink streaks	½"	upper elev.
stonecrop	Jun-Jul	white star cluster	⅓"	stream banks
strawberry	Mar-Jun	5 white petals	¾"	dry areas
sweet white violet	Apr-May	5 white petals	½"	stream banks
trillium (large)	Apr-May	3 white petals	3"	upper elev.
Virginia dayflower	Jun-Jul	2 blue petals	½"	sunny areas
winter cress	May-Jun	white cluster	1"	open fields

FISH

Whitetop Laurel Creek (Miles 17.8 to 27.3) may just be the finest trout stream in the Commonwealth of Virginia. Some may prefer meadow spring streams, like Mossy Creek in Augusta County. Others will argue that tail water rivers such as the Smith River and the Jackson River below the Gathright Dam produce consistently larger fish. But when measured in terms of wild trout, outstanding scenery, and limited competition from other fishermen, Whitetop Laurel is about as good as it gets.

The Commonwealth of Virginia seems to agree. Stream surveys conducted by the Department of Game and Inland Fisheries documented sufficient natural reproduction to provide quality fishing without stocking hatchery-raised trout. In 1984 Whitetop Laurel Creek became one of the first streams in Virginia with a nine-inch size limit and artificial lure restrictions in a specially regulated area.

Whitetop Laurel Creek's Special Regulation Area extends

upstream from the first trestle above Taylors Valley (Mile 23.2) to the confluence of Big Laurel Creek and Green Cove Creek at Creek Junction (Mile 27.3). This area extends southward along Green Cove Creek for another mile. In 1996 the size limit for trout creeled in the special regulation zone was increased to twelve inches. The significance of these fish management changes can be fully appreciated only when we recognize that Whitetop Laurel was certainly some of the first water in Virginia to be stocked with hatchery trout.

Shortly after the Civil War, as the timber industry spread across the eastern United States, fishermen began to notice a decline in trout populations. Unregulated logging practices and ensuing forest fires and erosion killed much of the stream-side and stream-floor vegetation and destroyed the watershed structures in these forests. The resulting decline in water quality left the region's streams unable to support its native brook trout.

After the Civil War, pioneering fishery biologists Seth Green and Robert Mather at the Federal Fish Hatchery (Cold Spring Harbor, New York) felt that the problem could be solved simply by putting fish back into the now trout barren waters. It was not understood at that time that self sustaining trout populations occur only when there is a suitable stream environment. They inadvertently promoted a philosophy that trout will populate a stream only if a hatchery truck unloads them there. They also began an intensive industry in trout breeding, seeking to produce a hybrid trout easily grown in hatcheries, early-maturing, and disease resistant. They began their research with strains of the brook trout and soon developed a fish that met these requirements. Unfortunately this trout was also small. Stocking these hybrids in streams where local brook trout populations still existed, the biologists introduced undesirable new characteristics into local populations.

Early fish culturists experimented with other species of trout, including the rainbow trout. In the 1880s, fertilized rainbow trout eggs from California were brought by ship around Cape Horn (since they could not survive train travel

Wytheville, Virginia, Federal Fish Hatchery, 1887. (Photo credit "Report of Operations at the Wytheville Station," 1889.)

Wytheville, Virginia, Federal Fish Hatchery, 1887. (Photo credit "Report of Operations at the Wytheville Station," 1889.)

TABLE I.—*Receipts of fish and eggs at Wytheville Station for the year ending June 30, 1887.*

Species.	Whence received.	Date.	Eggs.	Fish.
California trout	Central Station, by W. F. Page	Apr. 14		*5,000
Do	Central Station, by W. A. Dunnington	May 4		*3,000
	Collected at Wytheville Station		220,500	
	Total		220,500	8,000
Brook trout	Northville Station, by R. S. Johnson	Dec. 11		†193
Do	Northville Station, by express	Jan. 2	26,508	
Do	Richard E. Follett, Windham, Conn	Jan. 8	75,000	
Do	Central Station, by W. F. Page	Apr. 14		*5,000
	Total		101,508	5,193
Brown trout	Fred. Mather, Cold Spring Harbor, N. Y	Mar. 17	9,100	
Do	Central Station, by W. A. Dunnington	May 4		*3,000
Landlocked salmon	Chas. G. Atkins, Grand Lake Stream, Me	Mar. 13	50,000	
Red-eye perch	Peak Creek, Pulaski County, Va	Aug. 16		‡2,125
Do	do	Aug. 16		†58
Do	Reed Creek, Wythe County, Va	June 23		†19
	Total			2,202
Black bass	New River, Giles County, Va	Aug. 16		‡100
Do	Reed Creek, Wythe County, Va	June 23		†11
	Total			111
Carp (leather)	Central Station, Washington, D. C	Nov. 11, 20		‡3,000
Do	do	Mar. 1		†12
Do	do	Apr. 14		†2
Do	do	May 4		†3
Carp (scale)	do	Jan. 6		†450
Do	do	Apr. 14		†2
	Total			3,469
Tench	Central Station, Washington, D. C	Jan. 6		‡450
Do	do	Apr. 14		†2
	Total			452

* Fry. † Breeders. ‡ Yearlings.

TABLE II.—*Distribution of fish and eggs from Wytheville Station for the year ending June 30, 1887.*

Species.	Where sent.	Date.	Eggs.	Fish.
California trout	H. C. Parsons, Natural Bridge, Va	Aug. 11		*100
Do	M. C. Treiber, Staunton, Va	Aug. 11		*100
Do	North River, Weyer's Cave, Va	Aug. 11		*497
Do	A. Y. Stevens, Nashville, Tenn	Aug. 17		*100
Do	Edward D. Hicks, Nashville, Tenn	Aug. 17		*50
Do	J. D. Eads, Warrensburgh, Mo	Aug. 17		*75
Do	Tributary of Maramec River, Mo	Aug. 17		*925
Do	Tributary of Gasconade River, Mo	Aug. 17		*750
Do	Tributary of Osage River, Mo	Aug. 17		*950
Do	Tributary of Neosho River, Mo	Aug. 17		*925
Do	Tributary of White River, Ark	Aug. 17		*1,110
Do	George L. Harman, Olympic, Va	Aug. 20		*50
Do	do	Aug. 21		*50
Do	William Spangler, Speedwell, Va	Sept. 2		*20
Do	Stony Fork of Reed Creek, Wythe County, Va	Sept. 20		†100
Do	Eli F. Thomas, Grant, Va	Sept. 21		*25
Do	Headwaters of James River, Va	Sept. 23		*400
Do	Stony Fork of Reed Creek, Wythe County, Va	Sept. 23		*500
Do	Cacapon River, W. Va	Oct. 12		*400
Do	Henry Stewart, Highland, N. C	Oct. 19		*300
Do	D. B. Mackall, messenger, Washington, D. C	Nov. 7		*300
Do	J. W. Davis, Atkin's Tank, Va	Nov. 13		*25
Do	D. B. Mackall, messenger, Washington, D. C	Nov. 15		*250
Do	V. G. Shepard, Faber's Mills, Va	Nov. 15		*100
Do	Newton Simmons, messenger, Washington, D. C	Jan. 6		*225
Do	M. McDonald, Washington, D. C	Jan. 21	5,000	
Do	Max von dem Borne, Berneuchen, Germany	Jan. 24	10,000	
Do	N. Jeunet, Paris, France	Feb. 2	5,000	
Do	Deutsche Fischerei-Verein, Berlin, Germany	Feb. 7	15,000	
Do	do	Feb. 14	15,000	
Do	National Fish-Culture Association, London, England.	Feb. 21	10,000	

* Yearlings. † Two years or more.

Source: "Report of Operations at the Wytheville Station," 1889.

TABLE II.—*Distribution of fish and eggs from Wytheville Station, etc.*—Continued.

Species.	Where sent.	Date.	Eggs.	Fish.
California trout	M. V. Osborne, Cold Creek Hatchery, Ohio	Feb. 21	10,000	
Do	E. G. Shortlidge, Wilmington, Del	Feb. 21	5,000	
Do	E. H. Frishmuth, Philadelphia, Pa	Feb. 26	5,000	
Do	J. W. Hoxie & Co., Carolina, R. I	Feb. 26	3,000	
Do	Charles F. Hardie, New York, N. Y	Mar. 1	10,000	
Do	G. W. Delawder, Baltimore, Md	Mar. 1	5,000	
Do	Long Meadow Run, near Hagerstown, Md	Mar. 31		*622
Do	Almshouse Run, near Hagerstown, Md	Mar. 31		*622
Do	Rush Run, near Hagerstown, Md	Mar. 31		*622
Do	Walker's Run, near Hagerstown, Md	Mar. 31		*622
Do	South Fork of Reed Creek, Wythe County, Va	May 19		†65
Do	Holston River, near Marion, Va	May 20		*500
Do	Cove Creek, Wythe County, Va	May 24		*250
Do	Walker's Creek, Bland County, Va	May 27		*250
Do	North Fork of Reed Creek, Wythe County, Va	June 1		†100
Do	L. S. Allison, Wythe County, Va	June 20		*250
	Total		98,000	12,230
Brook trout	Long Meadow Run, near Hagerstown, Md	Mar. 31		‡622
Do	Almshouse Run, near Hagerstown, Md	Mar. 31		‡622
Do	Rush Run, near Hagerstown, Md	Mar. 31		‡622
Do	Walker's Run, near Hagerstown, Md	Mar. 31		‡622
Do	Cove Creek, Wythe County, Va	May 24		*250
Do	Walker's Creek, Bland County, Va	May 27		*250
Do	L. S. Allison, Wythe County, Va	June 20		*250
	Total			3,238
Lake trout	H. C. Parsons, Natural Bridge, Va	Aug. 11		*100
Do	M. C. Treiber, Staunton, Va	Aug. 11		*100
Do	Tributary of Gasconade River, Mo	Aug. 17		*50
Do	William Spangler, Speedwell, Va	Sept. 2		*20
Do	Eli F. Thomas, Grant, Va	Sept. 21		*25
Do	S. N. Hufford, Wytheville, Va	Oct. 9		*25
Do	D. B. Mackall, messenger, Washington, D. C	Nov. 15		*250
Do	do	Nov. 23		*600
Do	Newton Simmons, messenger, Washington, D. C	Jan. 30		*30
	Total			1,200
Landlocked salmon	Tributary of Shenandoah River, Staunton, Va	Aug. 11		*1,997
Do	South Fork of Shenandoah River, Waynesborough, Va.	May 19		*11,000
	Total			12,997
Red-eye perch	W. L. Bumgardner, Staunton, Va	Aug. 11		*25
Do	I. G. W. Steedman, St. Louis, Mo	Aug. 17		*60
Do	Cowpasture River, Bath County, Va	Sept. 23		*600
Do	Cacapon River, West Virginia	Oct. 12		*500
Do	W. O. Watson, Charlottesville, Va	Oct. 12		*200
Do	W. E. Grant, Grantland, Va	Oct. 15		*100
Do	D. B. Mackall, messenger, Washington, D. C	Nov. 7		*400
Do	V. G. Shepard, Faber's Mills, Va	Nov. 15		*100
Do	L. S. Pendleton, Frederick's Hall, Va	Nov. 15		*50
Do	Fred Mather, Cold Spring Harbor, N. Y	Dec. 12		*50
Do	Newton Simmons, messenger, Washington, D. C	Jan. 6		§6
Do	E. M. Robinson, messenger, Washington, D. C	Feb. 25		§12
	Total			2,103
Black bass	J. D. Eads, Warrensburgh, Mo	Aug. 17		*48
Carp (leather)	Ninety-one applicants in southwest Virginia and east Tennessee.			1,925
Carp (scale)	South Fork of Reed Creek, Wythe County, Va	Jan. 8		450
	Total			2,375
Tench	South Fork of Reed Creek, Wythe County, Va	Jan. 8		*450
Goldfish	Mrs. O. J. Smythe, Wytheville, Va	July 13		6
Do	J. C. Ewald, Paris, Tex	July 17		4
Do	Mrs. Emma W. Guy, Glade Spring, Va	Aug. 5		6
Do	Miss Daisy Bedford, Vicksburg, Miss	Aug. 10		6
Do	E. M. Robinson, Fayetteville, N. C	Dec. 21		8
Do	Charles Hancock, Wytheville, Va	Jan. 12		4
Do	J. G. Hollbrook, Wytheville, Va	Jan. 22		6
Do	Charles Ewald, Wytheville, Va	Mar. 6		4
Do	Hon. C. F. Trigg, Abingdon, Va			6
	Total			50

*Yearlings. †Two years or more. ‡Fry. §Breeders.

Source: "Report of Operations at the Wytheville Station," 1889.

through the deserts of the American Southwest) and propagated in several federal fish hatcheries in the eastern United States. The fish thrived in the hatcheries and later in the recovering streams. Fishermen liked the hard-fighting and leaping habits of this California transplant. Trout fisherman Ernest Hemingway made an astute observation: "Rainbow trout fishing is as different from brook trout fishing as prize fighting is from boxing."

Eggs of the rainbow trout, then referred to as the "California trout," were brought to Virginia in 1887. The federal government opened a fish hatchery in Wytheville to produce replacement trout for streams damaged by logging around the Southeast. A strain of rainbow trout developed at the Wytheville hatchery would eventually become the standard hatchery trout for the entire United States. Eggs from this hatchery were even exported to foreign countries. The Wytheville rainbow was noted for its exceptional growth in the hatchery environment, good return in the stream, and resistance to disease. Unlike the failed brook trout experi-

Trout are transferred to motorized rail cars for stocking in Whitetop Laurel Creek in the early 1950s. (Photo courtesy Virginia Department of Game and Inland Fisheries.)

Trout are stocked in Whitetop Laurel Creek in the early 1950s. (Photo courtesy Virginia Department of Game and Inland Fisheries.)

ment, it did not result in a stunted adult.

In those early years of trout restoration, before good roads and automobiles, trout were often transported by railroad. This meant that fish were taken to streams with reasonable rail access and dumped from the trestles directly into the water. The Virginia Creeper Railway's many crossings of Whitetop Laurel, Green Cove, and other creeks made it an excellent stocking stream. This stocking directly from railroad trestles continued through most of this century but was eventually replaced by special trucks. For many years the Virginia Creeper's stocking continued to be rail-oriented due to trucks with specially fitted steel wheels.

Rainbow trout have an urge to travel. They spread quickly up the tributaries of Whitetop Laurel Creek, taking over the water once home to the less aggressive brook trout. Brook trout, which require consistently cold and clear water, were greatly reduced in number by the damage inflicted on streams by poor logging practices. Competition with the rainbow trout for limited habitat was a further restraint which kept the brook trout population low. Brookies are at home in dark streams shaded by tall century-old hemlocks with thick carpets of moss along their banks. Perhaps in another fifty years this changing forest environment will again be the type of home where the brook trout can grow and prosper, but for now it is the silver colored rainbow that dominates these streams.

Another introduced species making its home in the Whitetop Laurel and some of its tributaries is the brown trout. The descendant of German and other European ancestors, the brown trout can now be found mixed among the rainbows. Adult brown trout were stocked in these streams for years, but a reproducing population was not successfully established. Then in the 1980s, Virginia's Department of Game and Inland Fisheries began stocking fingerling brown trout, which established self sustaining populations.

Brown trout can tolerate warmer water than either brook or rainbow trout. Although considered by both fishermen and biologists to be smarter and more aggressive than the other species, browns have not become dominant in these streams. Perhaps this reflects the improving quality of the stream as natural cold-water habitat.

Whitetop Laurel is a free stone stream. That means that the water chemistry or pH is slightly acidic. Streams that are alkaline, or have a high pH, tend to be more conducive to plant growth. The plants support insect life which in turn provides much of the food for the stream's fish. Whitetop Laurel is an excellent fly fishing steam but does not produce the very heavy May fly hatches that are sometimes seen on limestone meadow streams.

Predominant insects here are stone flies and caddis flies. Stone flies, a favorite food of large trout, may live as pupae in the stream for several years before hatching. Caddis flies are available to trout primarily in larval and pupal stages. Some caddis flies may hatch on the stream during any warm, non-winter month. Artificial flies that imitate these species will consistently take fish on Whitetop Laurel even in the warm months of July and August.

While Whitetop Laurel Creek is the favorite stream of many fishermen, its smaller tributary, Green Cove Creek (Miles 27.3 to 30.6), should not be overlooked. Stream surveys have shown an outstanding trout population with very little fishing pressure.

Nor should the portions of these streams outside the artificial lures section be ignored. Regular trout stockings occur here upstream from the special regulation area (Miles 28.3 to 30.6) and downhill from Taylors Valley (Miles 17.8 to 23.0) despite the fact that natural reproduction in these streams no longer makes this necessary. Although there is heavy pressure from bait fishermen, plenty of fish are available in these portions of Whitetop Laurel Creek.

Lake Fishing

Trout fishing may be the main fishing attraction along the Virginia Creeper Trail, but other kinds of fishing are available as well. Near Alvarado the trail crosses South Holston Lake at the confluence of the Middle and South forks of the Holston River (Mile 7.9). In this section of the trail, one may experience a wide variety of fishing opportunities.

The twenty-four-mile-long South Holston Lake is the easternmost lake in the Tennessee Valley Authority system. While the lake has an area of 7,580 acres, mostly in Tennessee, about six miles of its length is in Virginia, beginning at the trail's crossing. South Holston Lake is essentially a warm-water habitat, with good populations of smallmouth and largemouth bass. White bass are stocked in the reservoir, and each spring many schools of these bass ascend from the reservoir, pass under the Creeper Trail, and swim up the South Fork of the Holston to spawn. They seem to end their run at the first rapids near Alvarado (Mile 9.0). Fish in the two-to-four pound range are common. This run peaks when the dogwood trees are in bloom, around April.

Local fishermen pursue white bass with weighted "doll flies," minnows, and spinners. Very few fly-fishermen seem to go after these fish. Trying for these hard-fighting bass can be a frustrating experience. A common statement is: "You should have been here yesterday." The fickle fish will seem to have a taste for chartreuse doll flies when your tackle box is full of white and green models. Weather, water temperature, and water color—and probably many unidentified factors—affect the fish's movement. Fishermen who consistently go after these fish eventually find that obscure combination of the right lure at the right spot under the right conditions. At such time, a day's limit of twenty-five fish is an easy catch. Many fishermen then risk hernias and back injuries hauling home their catch.

White bass fishing is seldom a solitary experience. Because of easy public access to the spawning areas, when these fish are running, the white bass enthusiast will be joined by hundreds of fellow anglers along with their wives, children, and household pets. Old school buses converted into campers park along the river, and bird songs are drowned out by radios blaring country music and heavy metal rock. Hamburgers are cooked over open fires, and lots of beer is consumed by both the fishermen and their entourage. The old annual opening day for trout season was tame by comparison.

While the white bass is the most well-known of South Holston Lake's fish, there are other species worthy of attention. In 1986 walleyes were stocked in the reservoir, and they are now caught consistently here during the spring spawning run. Also introduced to the lake in recent years is the muskie. A Virginia record catch for this fish was caught near the Creeper Trail trestle (Mile 7.8) a few years ago. Other fish in the stream include sunfish, redeye, suckers, and an occasional trout.

Fishermen around America often lament for the "good old days" when water quality was good and there were plenty of fish. Fishing along the Virginia Creeper Trail is an exception—these are the good old days. Fishing here is probably the best it has been since the turn of the century when intensive logging began. The current quality of fishing is the result not of stocking, but of the gradual regrowth of the forest. Fishermen have every reason to believe that there are even better times ahead for those who fish these waters and learn their secrets.

BIRDS

"I'm pleased, pleased, pleased to meet'cha!" Or should I say, "I'm here to see Miss Beecher"? Have we lost you already? Both of these sentences are mnemonic representations of the song of the chestnut-sided warbler, one of the birds more commonly seen (or heard) along the Creeper Trail. This bird is particularly significant in the story of the trail since, at one time, it was perhaps the rarest bird species in North America—even more rare than the whooping crane or the California condor is today. John James Audubon saw only one of these birds in his lifetime!

What accounts for this dramatic change? While we often think of bird populations as relatively stable, that is seldom the case. Birds benefit and suffer from human impacts on their environment. Quail and bluebirds both thrive in traditional farmland areas, purple martins largely occupy houses built for them by people, and chimney swifts are comfortable in the smokestacks of our cities. When presented with habitat appropriate to their needs, birds (like other animals) readily fill the available niche. Just as often, however, the opposite occurs: habitat loss means the decline of a species, sometimes to the point of extinction. In the natural world, it is an ill wind indeed that doesn't blow some good.

The chestnut-sided warbler is a prime example. This particular bird thrives on land that is in transition from cleared land to second-growth forest. Thickets, briers, brush, and tangles are the places that this species calls home. According to Hal Harrison (in his book *Wood Warbler's World*), "the species is so closely allied to this habitat that it disappears from an area if trees become dominant and form a shady canopy."

Much of the forest surrounding the Virginia Creeper Trail was clear-cut between 1900 and 1930. What had been essentially virgin forest could never be home to the chestnut-sided warbler. The cleared land soon became covered with ideal habitat for this bird, however, and a population explosion followed. With this forest now maturing again, the bird is losing its habitat, and the cycle continues.

The thirty-four miles of trail between Abingdon and Whitetop Station pass through a wide variety of habitats due to varying elevations, sun exposures, forest types, and stream and land formations. The trail crosses a variety of active farms, including tobacco fields, pastures, vegetable gardens, cornfields, and hay fields as well as abandoned pastures and fields, growing thick with brush. Most of the trail is, however, surrounded by various stages of forest growth, including deep hemlock forest, laurel and rhododendron thickets, oak-hickory forest, mixed pine and hardwood forest, and even groves of eastern redcedar. The trail curves along rushing trout streams, wetlands, lakes, and slow-moving rivers. Such environmental variety makes possible a great diversity of bird species.

Seasons affect the kinds of birds seen along the trail. Neotropical migrants, which spend the colder half of the year (or more) in the Caribbean, Central America, and South America, come here to breed and may be sighted during the warmer months. These birds make up an important component of the Creeper Trail region's bird population. This group of birds includes the wood warblers and other colorful species such as the scarlet tanager and the orioles.

This region is also an important migratory route for raptors, or birds of prey, including hawks and eagles. Each year in fall and spring thousands of hawks, particularly broad-winged hawks, pass through here on their way north or south. Around Mount Rogers and Whitetop one might see golden eagles making their winter home. Another large and interesting bird resident is the raven, whose croaking call can be heard echoing across the treetops.

Streams and ponds along the trail sometimes provide homes or feeding stops for unusual species such as the great egret and the black-crowned night heron. Wood ducks and hooded mergansers are sometimes seen along beaver ponds near the trail, and the rattling call of the kingfisher is often heard as it hunts for prey along the many waterways. Those particularly interested in waterfowl may want to visit Bear Tree Lake, a few miles from the trail near Konnarock, where a wide variety of water birds can be sighted regularly, including pied-billed grebes, spotted sandpipers, and even common loons. In the evenings, along sections of the trail adjacent to streams, swallows and flycatchers are easily sighted as they feed on insects hatching there.

When passing along the trail, keep both an eye and an ear out for birds. A guide, such as the Peterson Field Guide to Eastern Birds, can help in identification. Developing recognition of birds endemic to this region can add a great deal to the Creeper Trail experience. It can also help build your appreciation of the role habitat plays in the region's constantly changing bird life.

Bird Checklist
Virginia Creeper Trail

- ☐ Common loon
- ☐ Pied-billed grebe
- ☐ Great blue heron
- ☐ Green heron
- ☐ Great egret
- ☐ Black-crowned night heron
- ☐ Canada goose
- ☐ Mallard
- ☐ American black duck
- ☐ Wood duck
- ☐ Lesser scaup
- ☐ Bufflehead
- ☐ Hooded merganser
- ☐ Turkey vulture
- ☐ Black vulture
- ☐ Sharp-shinned hawk
- ☐ Cooper's hawk
- ☐ Red-tailed hawk

- ☐ Red-shouldered hawk
- ☐ Broad-winged hawk
- ☐ Rough-legged hawk
- ☐ Golden eagle
- ☐ Northern harrier
- ☐ Peregrine falcon
- ☐ American kestrel
- ☐ Ruffed grouse
- ☐ Bobwhite
- ☐ Turkey
- ☐ American coot
- ☐ Killdeer
- ☐ Spotted sandpiper
- ☐ Common snipe
- ☐ Ring-billed gull
- ☐ Rock dove
- ☐ Mourning dove
- ☐ Yellow-billed cuckoo
- ☐ Barn owl
- ☐ Screech owl
- ☐ Great Horned owl
- ☐ Barred owl
- ☐ Saw-whet owl
- ☐ Whip-poor-will
- ☐ Common nighthawk
- ☐ Chimney swift
- ☐ Ruby-throated humming-bird
- ☐ Belted kingfisher
- ☐ Common flicker
- ☐ Pileated woodpecker
- ☐ Red-bellied woodpecker
- ☐ Red-headed woodpecker
- ☐ Yellow-bellied sapsucker
- ☐ Hairy woodpecker
- ☐ Downy woodpecker
- ☐ Eastern kingbird
- ☐ Great crested flycatcher
- ☐ Eastern phoebe
- ☐ Acadian flycatcher
- ☐ Eastern wood pewee
- ☐ Willow flycatcher
- ☐ Least flycatcher
- ☐ Horned lark
- ☐ Tree swallow
- ☐ Rough-winged swallow
- ☐ Barn swallow
- ☐ Cliff swallow
- ☐ Purple martin
- ☐ Blue jay
- ☐ Common raven
- ☐ Common crow
- ☐ Black-capped chickadee
- ☐ Carolina chickadee
- ☐ Tufted titmouse
- ☐ White-breasted nuthatch
- ☐ Red-breasted nuthatch
- ☐ Brown creeper
- ☐ House wren
- ☐ Winter wren
- ☐ Carolina wren
- ☐ Blue-gray gnatcatcher
- ☐ Golden-crowned kinglet
- ☐ Ruby-crowned kinglet
- ☐ Northern mockingbird
- ☐ Gray Catbird
- ☐ Brown thrasher
- ☐ American robin
- ☐ Wood thrush
- ☐ Hermit thrush
- ☐ Swainson's thrush
- ☐ Veery
- ☐ Eastern bluebird
- ☐ Cedar waxwing
- ☐ Loggerhead shrike
- ☐ European starling

- ☐ White-eyed vireo
- ☐ Yellow-throated vireo
- ☐ Solitary vireo
- ☐ Red-eyed vireo
- ☐ Black-and-white warbler
- ☐ Prothonotary warbler
- ☐ Worm-eating warbler
- ☐ Golden-winged warbler
- ☐ Blue-winged warbler
- ☐ Tennessee warbler
- ☐ Northern parula warbler
- ☐ Magnolia warbler
- ☐ Yellow warbler
- ☐ Cape May warbler
- ☐ Black-throated Blue warbler
- ☐ Yellow-rumped warbler
- ☐ Black-throated Green warbler
- ☐ Blackburnian warbler
- ☐ Chestnut-sided warbler
- ☐ Blackpoll warbler
- ☐ Ovenbird
- ☐ Kentucky warbler
- ☐ Louisiana waterthrush
- ☐ Common yellowthroat
- ☐ Yellow-breasted chat
- ☐ Hooded warbler
- ☐ Canada warbler
- ☐ American redstart
- ☐ House sparrow
- ☐ Eastern meadowlark
- ☐ Red-winged blackbird
- ☐ Rusty blackbird
- ☐ Orchard oriole
- ☐ Baltimore oriole
- ☐ Common grackle
- ☐ Brown-headed cowbird
- ☐ Scarlet tanager
- ☐ Northern cardinal
- ☐ Rose-breasted grosbeak
- ☐ Indigo bunting
- ☐ Evening grosbeak
- ☐ Purple finch
- ☐ House finch
- ☐ Pine siskin
- ☐ American goldfinch
- ☐ Red crossbill
- ☐ Rufous-sided towhee
- ☐ Dark-eyed junco
- ☐ Grasshopper sparrow
- ☐ Chipping sparrow
- ☐ Field sparrow
- ☐ White-crowned sparrow
- ☐ White-throated sparrow
- ☐ Swamp sparrow
- ☐ Song sparrow

MAMMALS

In the mountains, the quiet night is sometimes broken by the plaintive howl of a coyote. These are not the dry ridges of New Mexico or the mountains of Colorado, but the forests and farmlands of Southwest Virginia. Around 1990, the coyote arrived in Western Virginia, completing a march from the West and South that seems just as determined and successful (from the coyote's perspective) as Sherman's passage through Georgia more than a century before.

Now well established throughout Southwest Virginia, the coyote is seldom seen, usually detected only when it feeds on livestock or farm cats. This new resident is an indicator of dramatic changes in the region's wildlife and habitats during the past half-century.

Many factors contribute to the coyote's successful survival in Virginia. Perhaps the single most important factor is the area's increasing deer population, a population still recovering from near demise. By the late 1940s, the white-tailed deer in this region had been decimated by overhunting and habitat loss. Indeed, their numbers had probably never been large in Western Virginia since tall, mature forest is not a productive environment for deer, which browse on saplings and new plant growth. Native Americans burned some forests to increase the amount of large game in this area, but most of the land remained largely uninhabited by white-tailed deer.

However, the region is now a patchwork of fields and forests, including many young forests that grew after the logging era (1900 to 1930) and continued as farmland was abandoned in the 1930s. The resulting land transition provides excellent habitat for the whitetail and, therefore, for the coyote.

In the 1950s the Virginia Department of Game and Inland Fisheries began a trapping and stocking program that brought significant numbers of deer back to Southwest Virginia. Careful management of these herds through hunting regulation has resulted in a deer population explosion. One supporting factor is the previous extermination of wolves and mountain lions, once the primary predators controlling the deer herd. The opportunity for the coyote was clear. Ironically, roads and bridges that had opened the way west for pioneers and travelers later provided easy passage for the eastward-bound coyote. White-tailed deer are not the primary food of the coyote; however, the same habitat conditions that provide plant food for deer provide small animal

Elk

One of the first efforts to stock replacement wildlife in Virginia was the stocking of elk. In 1917, 150 elk were brought by rail from Yellowstone National Park to several mountainous counties in Virginia. This was done with financial help and encouragement from private sportsmen. The commonwealth's first elk hunting season ran from December 15 to 31, 1920. In 1922 Virginia had an elk herd estimated at 500 (approximately fifty in Washington County, seventy in Russell County, and the rest in Bland, Botetourt, Craig, Giles, and Warren counties). Indeed some were counted in Princess Anne County in Eastern Virginia. This experiment made Virginia the only state east of the Mississippi with huntable elk.

In 1935, another herd was brought in from Yellowstone. The grandfather of coauthor Ed Morgan remembered this later stocking in Giles County. The elk were brought on the train into Pearisburg, unloaded, and driven on the hoof into the mountains. The next morning the homesick elk reported back to the train station in the heart of town!

Elk survived in Virginia but did not thrive. Game officials suggest that food was the problem. Although their primary diet is normally grass, they were surviving mostly on browse here. Disease was also a problem since certain parasites common to white-tailed deer apparently thrive among elk.

Elk hunting continued in Virginia into the 1960s, with some hunters bringing in bulls weighing 900 pounds and sporting twelve-point racks. The last wild elk was seen in Virginia in 1970.

It is highly likely that herds of elk will be reestablished in Virginia in the near future. Virginia game officials have agreed to explore the possibility of stocking elk. Pennsylvania now has a herd of 400 animals. Starting in 1997 Kentucky game officials plan to stock as many as 100 elk over a three year period in strip mined lands just across Virginia's borders. These large, free ranging animals do not concern themselves with artificial boundaries such as state lines, and they can be expected to roam into Virginia.

Beaver signs on the Creeper Trail can be seen near Mile 29.0 and elsewhere. (Photo by Edward H. Davis.)

food for coyotes. Of course, no coyote would pass up a deer if available! The coyote's presence certainly indicates that human influence in the local ecosystem has not led to human control.

Another regional mammal population currently on the rise is the black bear. Its habitat, the mature forest, has been so diminished in the twentieth century that it was absent from almost every part of the Southwest Virginia mountains. An exception was land now included in the Clinch Mountain Wildlife Management Area. In the late 1980s, Virginia wildlife biologists recognized that much of the forest in the Mount Rogers National Recreation Area (NRA) had recovered enough to support black bears. Problem bears in the Shenandoah National Park were captured and relocated to the Mount Rogers NRA. A portion of Southwest Virginia south of Interstate 81 was designated as a bear sanctuary (hunting prohibited). The result has been the successful reestablishment of a predator to its natural home.

A third important area mammal story is that of the beaver. These aquatic animals were so heavily trapped for their valuable fur in the 1800s that beaver became locally extinct. In 1911, the last known beaver in Virginia was killed in Dinwiddie County. As forests recovered from logging, the beaver returned. They extend their range by following streams in search of suitable habitat, bringing many beaver colonies into Southwest Virginia. Along Whitetop Laurel Creek, one can see gnawed stumps of trees, the obvious mark of beavers. To find their dams, one has to go farther into the forest where beavers reside along several tributaries. An exception is the group of small dams near Green Cove, at about Mile 28.9.

Other mammals once important to local ecosystems include the elk, red wolf, cougar, and bison. The cougar (also called mountain lion or panther) might live in the mountains near the Creeper Trail. Every year there are reports of cougars in Virginia's mountains, especially around the Shenandoah National Park and the counties bordering West Virginia (though the large territory required by a cougar means most of those reports are probably erroneous). Red wolves were reintroduced by state biologists in North Carolina and Tennessee and seem to be thriving. In the 1700s, the woods bison ranged over much of the eastern United States, probably because Native Americans burned enough forest to let bison herds find grass and migrate through mountain gaps. Indeed, early settlers used old bison pastures for grazing cattle and hogs.

Now the only bison in this area are the few imported from the west and raised for meat like domestic beef cattle. Still, if other large wild animals (like the black bear) can return to the natural areas of our region, perhaps the bison will also.

Large game animals such as deer and black bear will grab the attention of trail users, but many more kinds of small animals can also be found here. Following is a list of most of the common mammals, but there are also many snakes, salamanders, frogs, and lizards. Certain stretches of the trail are especially likely places. For example, the large forests along the highest ten miles of the trail (Mile 23.0 to 33.0) see fewer humans—and humans, therefore, see more animals. Bear and bobcat are extremely shy and are able to hear you long before you see them, so only the most patient and lucky ever glimpse them. Some animals, including squirrels, groundhogs, and chipmunks, are sighted because they are active in the daytime. Other animals are rarely seen because they are active only at night and sometimes at dawn or dusk. These include bats and flying squirrels.

Hunting is permitted on National Forest lands (approximately Mile 17.8 to 22.5, and 24.0 to 29.0) for those with a special stamp from the Forest Service. Virginia further regulates hunting in the commonwealth, and some counties require that big-game hunters purchase damage stamps. Most of the private land along the trail is posted. Those planning to hunt along the trail should purchase the necessary license and stamps, and adhere to all regulations. Firing across the trail is prohibited at all times. Hunting seasons and bag limits in Virginia vary greatly depending on the game.

Mammals Checklist
Virginia Creeper Trail

Mammal	Max. wt.	Habitat	Main food
☐ bat, big brown	0.1 lb.	fields/edges	insects
☐ bear, black	600 lbs.	forest	fruit, nuts, fish, insects
☐ beaver	70 lbs.	stream	bark, twigs
☐ bobcat	35 lbs.	forest	small animals
☐ chipmunk, eastern	0.5 lb.	forest/edges	seeds, nuts, berries
☐ coyote	50 lbs.	forest/edges	rodents, fruit, deer
☐ deer, white-tailed	250 lbs.	forest/edges	various plants
☐ fox, red	15 lbs.	forest/edges	almost anything
☐ groundhog	20 lbs.	fields/edges	various plants
☐ mink	5 lbs.	streams/lakes	fish
☐ mouse, field	0.2 lb.	fields	seeds, berries, grass
☐ mouse, white-footed	0.1 lb.	fields/forest	seeds, berries, grass
☐ muskrat	5 lbs.	streams/lakes	plants
☐ opossum	15 lbs.	forest/edges	almost anything
☐ rabbit, cottontail	4 lbs.	fields/edges	various plants
☐ raccoon	25 lbs.	forest/edges	almost anything
☐ skunk, striped	10 lbs.	forest/edges	small animals
☐ squirrel, flying	0.5 lb.	forest	nuts
☐ squirrel, fox	3 lbs.	forest	nuts
☐ squirrel, gray	2 lbs.	forest	nuts
☐ squirrel, red	1 lb.	forest	nuts

L. C. Hassinger stands beside one of the last of the giant trees in Pennsylvania, cut in 1898 just eight years before the Hassingers brought their sawmill and twenty-five Swedish families to Southwest Virginia and built the town of Konnarock, stimulating the success of the Virginia Creeper Railway. (Photo courtesy of Martin Hassinger.)

CHAPTER TWO: HISTORY

THE VIRGINIA CREEPER RAILWAY

When railroads were built into Southwest Virginia and Northwest North Carolina just before the Civil War, the higher mountains near the intersection of Virginia, Tennessee, and North Carolina were seen as too rugged for development. There were old trails, some of them Indian trails, winding along the creeks up into those mountains, but the deep hardwood forests were mostly a remote haven for scattered families and individuals who liked it that way. Indeed, many homesteaders in this marginal section of the Blue Ridge Mountains did not hold clear title to the land on which they lived. In the regional and national economic sense, these were lands that almost nobody wanted.

Post-Civil War industrial expansion brought this region into focus for numerous speculators seeking mineral wealth. The most well-financed was a retired Civil War officer, "General" J. D. Imboden, who believed that iron ore found in this area would support a major steel industry. He selected the small farming community of Mock's Mill in southwestern Washington County, Virginia, as the best site for a new industrial center, incorporating the town with the new name *Damascus* in 1886. Imboden chose this name to spur on the town's hoped-for destiny as a steel center since Damascus, Syria, had once been the steel capital of the Mediterranean.

Some justification existed for this iron/steel speculation. From the 1870s to the 1890s, iron was successfully mined in some nearby valleys and was processed in rather simple furnaces, called "bloomeries." Across the Tennessee line, just a few miles south of Damascus, one can visit the town of Laurel Bloomery as well as Furnace Creek, named for facilities built there over a century ago. But much larger iron ore deposits were discovered and accessed by rail in the midwestern states, so developing the scant minerals of this region became economically unfeasible.

Yet hopes were high in 1887, when speculators organized the Southwest Virginia Mining Company. The Abingdon Coal and Iron Railroad Company (AC&IRC) was incorporated, as well, to reap the profit involved in transporting the ore. Virginia gave this corporation the right to build and operate a railroad connecting to the well-established Norfolk & Western Railroad linking Bristol and Abingdon with Roanoke and points east. The new company spent two years securing funds and right-of-way. Even then, manual labor was done at minimum cost by African-American convicts from a Virginia state prison. According to sources in the Norfolk & Western files, some of these men died while working and their bodies were buried in the right-of-way, apparently in unmarked graves. These men deserve credit for moving a vast amount of earth and stone to create the sixteen-mile, gently sloping path between Abingdon and Damascus.

With the national economy in a recession and the hopes for a successful steel industry fading fast, the railroad's financial backers turned elsewhere. With no bridges built (fifteen were needed) and no tracks installed, the AC&IRC folded in 1893. All assets were taken over in 1894 by a new company, the Virginia Western Coal and Iron Railroad Company. This company suffered from a similar lack of funds, so no track was laid during the next four years. A casual observer standing on the grade in 1898 might have concluded that this "railroad" had no future, pointing as it did into the Iron Mountains that had no viable iron resources.

However, in that year one keen observer stood on the grade and saw something other speculators had not seen. Wilton E. Mingea, freight agent in Roanoke for the Norfolk & Western Railroad, knew about the high demand for lumber which accompanied the construction of railroads and homes around the country. He knew about the exhaustion of virgin timber reserves in New York and Pennsylvania. He also knew that some of eastern North America's last large virgin timber was in the mountains of Washington and Grayson counties,

A steam drill is used during construction of Virginia Creeper Railway, 1910. (Photo courtesy of Martin Hassinger.)

just a few miles east and south of Damascus. And, finally, he knew that a railroad reaching that timber could bring one of the highest returns on investment available at the time. Meanwhile, the Virginia Western Coal and Iron Railway Company went bankrupt, leaving its assets available and cheap.

For a good price, Mingea bought right-of-way deeds with financing from timber companies and real estate developers (especially the Douglas Land Company). After building bridges and laying track for two years, the Virginia-Carolina Railroad went into action on February 7, 1900, as its first train steamed along from Abingdon to Damascus.

As the century began, Damascus became the entry point for a considerable new transportation network. To support nearby logging activities, two narrow-gauge extensions—the Beaverdam Creek Railroad and the Thayer & Laurel Railroad—were quickly built southward from Damascus. Additional logging transport was done with teams of oxen and draft horses harnessed to wagons loaded daily with massive hemlock, chestnut, white pine, yellow poplar, and oak logs. Although most virgin timber was still far from railroad access, Mingea shipped out enough timber to record considerable profit in the first years. In 1905, for example, his short-line railroad had a net profit of $32,000.

In 1906, other ambitious and well-financed entrepreneurs arrived. Three Hassinger brothers—L. C., John and Will—brought their large-band sawmill and timber management team from Forest County, Pennsylvania, and purchased about 35,000 acres of land to work here. Much of that land was on the area's highest elevations, around the broad slopes of Whitetop Mountain. The Hassinger Company built its own town near the settlement of Azen, about fourteen miles east of Damascus, and Mingea and Hassinger cooperated to extend a connector line of the Virginia, Carolina and Southern Railroad into Hassinger's logging areas. In the first five months of 1906, about eight miles of this extension were completed through the narrow gorge to Taylors Valley, and then stretched beyond to climb the crooked stream valley. The *Damascus Blade* dated March 3, 1907, carried this

Manual labor was used to construct the bed for the Virginia Creeper Railway, here showing the railbed west of Green Cove in 1912. (Photo courtesy of Martin Hassinger.)

description: "The Hassinger Lumber Company here owns the timber rights to the largest and finest tract of timberland in the entire South. For six miles along their railroad...they own every foot of timber.... The trees are of magnificent proportions, especially along the sides of Whitetop, where they tower to a dizzying height and are as straight as a ship's mast."

On October 8, 1907, the railroad linked the Hassinger company town (now called Konnarock) to Damascus, and logging took on a fever pitch. Thereafter, the company cut an amazing fifteen million board feet of lumber in a typical year. *National Lumber Magazine* reported in 1912 that Washington County, Virginia, produced more lumber than any county in the United States and more than the entire state of Pennsylvania. By far the largest producer in the county, the Hassinger Lumber Company built 190 miles of their own narrow-gauge track during the next few years, reaching many coves of mature forest on and near Whitetop Mountain.

By century's end, railroading was common throughout most of Virginia's other sections. By 1856 the Norfolk & Western line was complete across Southwest Virginia, connecting Roanoke (then called Big Lick) with Bristol. But here was a sparsely settled frontier—a narrow, 350-mile long stretch of Blue Ridge Mountains, where forty more years would pass with no railroad. Wagon roads were hard to find and harder to use. So some traditional Appalachian culture survived longer along this frontier than elsewhere. Interviews with older people from Whitetop Mountain reveal a wide knowledge of medicinal herbs and nineteenth-century farming methods. Log homes and barns were still built using old techniques and styles.

Once the steel rails were laid down, however, these relic cultural traits began to disappear at a startling pace. Many families came out of the mountain hollows into Damascus and its satellite villages for jobs in the lumber mills. Mountain farm families, once isolated, were now tied by wood and steel to the national economy.

Damascus, the largest incorporated town in this timber zone, saw rapid industrial growth. The combination of virgin timber and regular railroad service made Damascus a boom town. Further adding to the competitive advantages of this timber town was its location relative to Atlantic seaboard cities—all other large virgin timber stands were farther south and west. Several northern investors came to Damascus. Thayer-Clement, Inc., a New York door and sash manufacturer, relocated here to use the high-quality white pine and other woods cut locally. Tanneries and extract plants, mostly from Pennsylvania's exhausted timber regions, also relocated here to take advantage of the bark production. All along the railroad between Abingdon and Damascus, sidings were built to allow small local sawmills to load trains with lumber. Trail users can still find faint traces of sidings at Alvarado, Drowning Ford, Delmar, and Laureldale. As the backbone of the local cash economy, the Virginia-Carolina Railway continued to make good money. In 1909, this company reported a net profit of $36,000.

Mingea, now racing Hassinger to expand southward and eastward through the mountains toward the sea, had big dreams. This front-page story from Abingdon's *Virginia Republican* dated June 23, 1911, tells the tale:

Extension of V.-C. to Coast is Probable

Monday morning after the arrival of the N & W train from Bristol there pulled out from the station here, over the Virginia-Carolina Railway, a special train, consisting of an engine, N & W cabin car, box car and one coach. On this train were a lot of bright looking young men in khaki suits, with several older men and a large number of engineer's transits, levels, etc. The box car was closed, but it was said to be loaded with camp equipment. Nobody outside of the railroad people knew what all this meant, but it was reported that W. E. Mingea, President of the V-C Ry., has secured $300,000 and will begin at once to extend the road to Wilkesboro, N.C. The interest was intensified when, as Engineer Thompson was given the "high ball" and as the train pulled out, someone sang out "Off for Wilkesboro!"

This is the way the Virginian (formerly the Tidewater) Railroad was started: H. H. Rogers' chief engineers, engineering equipment and camp outfit left at several points and went to work, and we see the result now in the great trunk line from the Ohio River to Hampton Roads....

The extension of the Virginia-Carolina would mean much for Abingdon, Bristol and Washington and Grayson counties in Virginia; for North Carolina and the counties traversed the advantages will be beyond computation.

Expanding his operations required Mingea to share control of his dream. In 1911, he allowed Norfolk & Western to assume some financial control of the railroad. With the increased funds available for construction, he then expanded across Whitetop Station's high gaps and into the New River watershed. In 1913, Mingea received North Carolina's per-

Bridge rebuilt after 1916 flood washed out eighteen bridges. (Photo courtesy of Martin Hassinger.)

mission to build his line through Lansing, West Jefferson, and Smethport to Elkland (now Todd) on Ashe County's southern edge.

By July 1914, this section of the Virginia-Carolina Railway was complete at its peak length of seventy-six miles. The Virginia-Carolina Railway would never be connected to another line; a major timber company refused to sell a right-of-way across their 75,000 acres. From 1915 through 1924, traffic was as heavy as the line would allow: six freights and two passenger trains each day. Local residents were very proud; to them the miles of steel track and the 325-ton steam engines were marvels of human endeavor, linking them to the world at large. Some people remained skeptical, however. Author Lloyd Lewis, whose relatives helped build the railroad, tells the story of an old aunt who refused to join her family on an excursion, saying she preferred to stay on "dry land."

No known record exists of a passenger killed on the Virginia Creeper, yet the line was constantly under threat from the forces of nature. Built with an exceptional number of bridges and trestles (100 of them), because crisscrossing the winding streams with wood was cheaper than dynamiting and filling, the Virginia Creeper was vulnerable. Maintenance crews provided welcome jobs to many local men, but repairs from floods and fires limited the railroad's profit. By 1912, the hard future of this tenuous system was becoming evident. The railroad reported a net profit of less than $8,000 that year. Flooding destroyed several railroad bridges in 1916, and a forest fire caused further damage in 1917. Volunteer fire departments, with support from the Hassinger Company, worked especially hard in dry autumn months to fight fires and reduce fire risk. While the Hassinger Company had an excellent record of fire risk reduction through careful logging practices, other companies and the railroad itself sometimes caused forest fires which burned hundreds of acres. In addition, some floods were linked to slopes left barren by logging companies. Both the frequency and force of these floods were to increase.

Despite these problems (and a national railroad crisis from 1913 to 1917), Norfolk & Western recognized the potential benefits of controlling all rail traffic in the region. Mingea was bought out; and beginning in 1916, Norfolk & Western gradually acquired the entire line. Eventually Mingea and the other stockholders were paid two million dollars, and on July 1, 1919, the Virginia-Carolina Railway became N & W's "Abingdon Branch." Mingea told local reporters he was ready for time to study and travel.

The 1920s were the golden age along the Abingdon Branch. This decade began with brisk rail traffic: logging, tanning, and wood-product manufacturing were well established in the towns along the line. Damascus had nearly all the same services as Abingdon, its older and larger rival. Even cultural activities flourished in these mountains that had been virtual wilderness a generation before.

Above Whitetop Station, an annual Whitetop Folk Festival was begun, drawing crowds from many miles away. Although this festival may have originated in an effort to preserve local culture, elderly residents now remember these

Workers stand on cribbing they have built to hold a dirt road bed in 1916. (Photo courtesy of Martin Hassinger.)

festivals simply as great times. One man recalls riding the train home from the festival, "feeling on top of the world."

As early as 1924, the unsustainable nature of local logging practices was evident. The largest stands of high-quality timber had been clear-cut, and companies began to leave. That year saw rail traffic reduced to three freights and two passenger trains a day. Switching to lumber retailing, the Hassinger Company built a large store in Bristol and, on

White pine logs are loaded for export to English ship builders in 1916. (Photo courtesy of Martin Hassinger.)

The company town of Konnarock, Virginia, is seen in 1916, about the height of logging activity around Whitetop Mountain and the year Norfolk & Western began acquiring the "Virginia Creeper" Railway. (Photo courtesy of Martin Hassinger.)

Large logs roll from the train into the Konnarock Millpond, circa 1920. (Photo courtesy of Martin Hassinger.)

Logging was very intense, so that most of the trees that could be reached by the system of narrow-gauge tracks were shipped out within twenty years of the arrival of Hassinger Lumber Company. A narrow-gauge train with log loader is seen circa 1926. (Photo courtesy of Martin Hassinger.)

Christmas Eve 1928, shut down the Konnarock operation. As the logging boom now ended, the railroad built for it would register no profit during the fifty years that followed.

In 1929, daily traffic was two freights and one passenger train. Spring rains in the following year brought the worst flood ever along the line, downing so many bridges that the railroad did not run for six months. The branch to Konnarock was abandoned by N & W, then in 1933 the section from West Jefferson to Elkland was abandoned, reducing the branch's length to fifty-five miles.

During the Depression, trains "mixed," carrying freight, mail, and passengers. A typical train would have a steam engine, coal tender, three box cars, three flat cars, two passenger cars, and a caboose. Some of the famous loads carried out of Abingdon bound for West Jefferson included cattle salvaged from the Dust Bowl disaster on the Great Plains and stone for construction of the Blue Ridge Parkway. Some lesser-known loads included many box cars of rhododendron bushes destined for landscaping businesses in the Northeast and medicinal herbs gathered out of the second-growth forest by local people for a little cash each year. Tanneries con-

THE "VIRGINIA CREEPER" NAME

The "V-C" line became affectionately known as the Virginia Creeper in the 1930s or 1940s. Exactly when and how, no one knows. But here are two popular explanations as to why: First, the track followed such a curvaceous course that it was likened to the ubiquitous native vine called Virginia Creeper. Other railroads of this type were called "pea vines" by local people for the same reason. Second, a train had to negotiate such sharp curves and steep grades (3% approaching Whitetop Station) that it could only creep slowly up and down the mountain. Perhaps the originator(s) of the term liked the double meaning as well as the use of the "V-C" initials. Whatever the origin, the choice has certainly added to the romantic image of this particular railroad.

tinued to operate, as did smaller logging operations, but this branch of the N & W consistently lost money, only three decades after it was built.

Now the mountains and their significance were changing dramatically. The steep cut-over lands east and south of Damascus, which had not been replanted with quality trees, were worth little in the short term. Timber companies sold this land to the federal government as part of the new National Forest system. Back at the turn of the century, when the area's virgin timber so impressed visitors, a Congressional bill was introduced to create a federal forest reserve. This bill was still in committee in 1907 when the cutting began. Thirty years later, the same land—but a much younger forest—became part of the Jefferson National Forest, including about sixteen miles of Virginia Creeper right-of-way.

Local residents were given free permits to gather materials from the National Forest. For example, in the twelve months preceding July 1, 1934, the local district gave out permits for a total of 4,385 cords of fuelwood; 662,000 board feet of

This narrow-gauge 30-ton Lima Shay locomotive was one used in Hassinger operations around Whitetop in 1926. (Photo courtesy of Martin Hassinger.)

This 120-ton Lima Shay locomotive carried most Virginia Creeper traffic for the Hassinger Lumber Company in 1926. (Photo courtesy of Martin Hassinger.)

A 120-ton Lima Shay wrecked when a trestle collapsed in 1927. (Photo courtesy of Martin Hassinger.)

lumber; 3,850 posts; and an unknown amount of fruit, shrubs, and plants. February of 1934 had been the coldest in thirty years, and fuelwood was greatly needed. These forest products, many of which were carried locally on the railroad, helped support a lot of rural families during the Depression. Removal of "dead and down material" from the forest was encouraged by the Forest Service in part because it reduced the risk of fire.

The Depression and the closure of Hassinger Lumber operations weren't as tragic for local residents around Whitetop Mountain as one might imagine. Many of these people were semi-subsistence farmers with only partial dependence on the cash economy. Around Green Cove, one can meet older residents who never once rode the train, who grew up uninterested in national holidays, and who report that they did not notice the Depression at all. For them the phrase "this country" refers not to the United States, but to the section of these mountains where they were raised. Even "Virginia" and "Southern Appalachia" are too large for their affections. Despite the Depression and the absence of the Hassinger Company after 1928, the community of Konnarock continued to support itself through local food production and the help of a Lutheran mission school.

Many mountain families became dependent on the modern industries brought into the mountains by the Virginia Creeper. Not surprisingly, for every person that stayed in this area, two or three migrated out. The steel rails, heralded as a means to modernity and economic prosperity in the 1920s, began to carry the bright young people out of the mountains in the 1930s. Adding further insult to the railroad's fading era, the federal government paved a highway through the area and, ironically, Eleanor Roosevelt visited the Whitetop Festival in 1932 by automobile.

The automobile changed the meaning of the railroad in the 1930s. Although most people did not own a motorized vehicle, residents along the line often had access to a car or truck. Even the poorest could hitchhike. So passenger train service became nonessential except to a few, remaining an important luxury. However, those seeking the urbane luxury portrayed in magazines and movies couldn't help but notice the lack of comfort on the Abingdon Branch. Cinders, rough jolts, and lack of good heat in winter made the train a poor choice compared to a 1936 Ford, once the roads were reliable. Of course, when taking a long journey, the train was still an affordable choice, and one could catch an air-conditioned Pullman car at the depot in Abingdon as early as 1934. Overall, however, for most residents here the mail became the only reason to anticipate the train's arrival.

The 1940s saw an even greater population decline in the area as many people moved to new factory jobs. With the war economy drawing young people to cities like Radford and Norfolk, Damascus lost its industry, as wood resources were scarce and tanneries had switched away from bark as their main input. Federal highways made truck traffic very competitive for the freight transport, allowing factories to locate in more diverse locations. Ironically, part of U.S. Highway 58 is built on an old railroad bed graded by Hassinger Lumber Company.

The Virginia Creeper continued to provide vital service when heavy snow blocked the roads. In 1942, snow fell just as Mrs. Wade Weaver of Whitetop was approaching her baby's due date. Home births were still the norm in this region, and experienced midwives like Sister Sophie Moeller were local heroes. But Mrs. Weaver became quite ill and could not give birth at home. News of this was brought to Abingdon on a train, which then carried a doctor to Whitetop. The train waited while he went the five miles farther to her cabin. She was placed on a sledge which was pulled through the snow back to Whitetop Station. Mrs. Weaver safely gave birth to a baby boy after the train carried her down to Abingdon's Johnston Memorial Hospital.

Such railroad dependence was fading fast, and the 1950s saw passenger railroads closed down throughout the United States. Yet this was a rather stable time for the Virginia Creeper. Although traffic was reduced to one mixed train a day in 1954, these trains kept a regular schedule up and

Leaving AM except Sun.	Station		Arriving PM except Sun.
7:20	Abingdon		5:15
7:32	Watauga		5:00
7:45	Barron		4:45
8:12	Damascus		4:20
8:39	Taylors Valley		4:02
8:54	Arr. Creek Junction		3:48
9:27	Lv. Creek Junction		3:16
9:42	Green Cove		3:01
9:52	Whitetop Gap		2:50
10:27	Tuckerdale		2:16
11:03	West Jefferson		1:40
11:39	Bowie		1:10
12:05 Ar.	Elkland	Lv.	12:40

For the Konnarock Branch:

PM	AM			PM	AM
3:17	8:55	Lv Creek Junction	Ar	3:47	9:26
3:32	9:10	Ar Konnarock	Lv	3:33	9:11

This 1915 schedule appeared in the May 30 *Journal Virginian* (Abingdon, Virginia).

down the mountain. The stability was due partly to the area's legacy of isolation: Norfolk & Western knew that train service was crucial to many local residents since there was still no through road between Abingdon and West Jefferson.

For some families living uphill from Damascus, time was standing still. At Green Cove Station, Mrs. Adele Edwards sold bag lunches to train passengers as she had done for years. Orders were placed by telegraph from Abingdon and Damascus. For fifty cents one could get a ham biscuit or fried chicken, a tart or apple pie, and a pop bottle filled with hot coffee.

When such a nostalgic place attracts the attention of someone from the national media, it must be on its last legs.

Leaving AM except Sun.	Station		Arriving PM except Sun.
7:30	Abingdon		3:40
7:55	Alvarado		3:11
8:20	Damascus		2:46
8:25	Laureldale		2:36
8:40	Taylors Valley		2:21
8:58	Creek Junction		2:06
9:19	Green Cove		1:51
9:54	Whitetop		1:36
10:16	Nella		1:11
10:29	Tuckerdale		12:59
10:39	Lansing		12:49
10:44	Bina		12:39
10:51	Warrensville		12:31
11:01	Smethport		12:21
11:15 Ar.	W. Jefferson	Lv.	12:15

This schedule was published as a brochure by Norfolk & Western in 1954.

In 1956, New York photographer O. Winston Link came to see one of America's last steam engines still doing regular service on the Virginia Creeper line. He made many photos of the Virginia Creeper, and several were published with a story in the July 1957 issue of *Trains* magazine. Link's highly professional photos drew a surge of visitors to the Creeper. When Norfolk & Western later announced that its steam locomotives would be replaced by diesels, many railroad buffs joined local people in protest.

The basis for this local fondness toward the Virginia Creeper Railway may be due to its constancy over two generations. Compare the two schedules shown above.

Despite some differences in these schedules and changes brought by the intervening world, forty years passed with little change in the Virginia Creeper. Departures and arrivals of friends and relatives, the mail, the smoke and steam, and the sounds of the train whistle and the churning locomotive were nearly daily constants for the thousands of women, men, and children living within a few miles of those rails.

Sentiment cannot resist the shifting economy, however, and in December 1957, diesel locomotives began pulling trains on the Abingdon Branch. Freight would continue to run, but the last regularly scheduled passenger train made its circuit on May 20, 1962. (A short section in North Carolina had service until late the next year, due to a law dealing with isolation from automobile access.) Special "Autumn Leaf" excursions were mounted for a few years in the 1960s, as tourists (and locals) sought to "experience the past" and see the mountains and the now-reviving forest.

Norfolk & Western now sought a buyer for the Creeper. Some visionaries spread hopes of an amusement park, similar to Tweetsie Railroad in Blowing Rock, North Carolina. But unlike Tweetsie, the Abingdon Branch had the liability of many wooden trestles under constant threat from flood, fire and decay. Even photographer O. W. Link, who had expressed his love of the Virginia Creeper, was courted as a buyer, but he found projected maintenance costs to be prohibitive. The N & W found no takers.

Hearings before the Interstate Commerce Commission were held in West Jefferson in May of 1973, in which N & W explained the costs of keeping the railroad in safe operating condition. The annual maintenance cost estimate was $163,000, with an additional $300,000 for repairs long overdue on rails and ties. The company presented records showing their losses in recent years, as well as repair cost in the event flooding occurred like that in 1940.

Many local residents attended the hearings to argue for continuing railroad service, citing the vitality of their communities and the tourism potential surrounding the railroad. The ICC decided on April 5, 1976, to abandon the Abingdon Branch effective April 1, 1977.

A council of local governments, with support from state officials, met in Ashe County to organize a promotion drive. In January 1977 this group produced a feasibility study showing that the traffic could be increased (specifically from

Walking or riding the Creeper Trail today we ought to remember with gratitude the workers who made the gentle roadbed mostly by hand, shown here near Green Cove, 1912. (Photo courtesy of Martin Hassinger.)

This retired caboose is now an information booth at the Damascus Town Park - Mile 16.0. (Photo by Edward H. Davis.)

seven to twenty-four freight loads per mile per year) to make the railroad profitable. The same report showed that a tourist railroad might earn money but would have to carry many more passengers than the "Autumn Leaf" excursions. Washington County officials, in a burst of optimism, made an offer to buy the whole railroad operation for $20,000, but Norfolk & Western was waiting for a much higher offer.

So the last train ran on March 31, 1977. A fan of the railroad, Lloyd Lewis, was there that day and later wrote an article for *Trains* magazine in which he crafted this wistful image of the event: "Perhaps the most telling cameo was the little boy who stood with his dog at trackside on the outskirts of West Jefferson, waving with all his might at the last train. Engineer Lester blew for the crossing and threw in a few more blasts for the youngster. Box cars and empty pulpwood flats rumbled past him. And when the caboose came, the brakeman tossed off a piece of candy. The little fellow picked up the candy and kept waving, waving goodbye forever to an American 'down-home' stretch of rural railroading...."

On April 23, 1977, Norfolk & Western sold all the track as scrap metal, as well as bridges and trestles, to Bill Fry of the Chicago Contracting Company for $402,000. Fry was under contract to complete removal by April 23, 1978. The Virginia Creeper Railway was about to be erased from the landscape.

THE VIRGINIA CREEPER NATIONAL RECREATION TRAIL

As the Creeper was shutting down, discussion emerged within the Washington County Board of Supervisors about trying to keep the railroad running as a locally owned venture. In the summer of 1977, Dave Brilhart, M.D., a member of the county Planning Commission, brought forward a *Washington Post* article about making trails out of abandoned right-of-way corridors. Several successful "rail-to-trail" conversions had occurred in the early '70s in Wisconsin. Inspired by these stories, Dr. French Moore, Jr. (then Abingdon's Vice-Mayor) and a few other supporters investigated and decided to pursue the idea. However, the Chicago Contracting Company was preparing to remove not only the steel rails but also the bridges and trestles which would be necessary for a trail. French Moore and his associates quickly requested and obtained a delay from Norfolk & Western in removing the trestles and steel bridges.

For the North Carolina section of the railroad, abandonment had meant immediate return of right-of-way to landowners along the route. This return was according to the following clause in the deeds required by North Carolina law: "in event of railroad closure, all right-of-way would automatically return to the landowners or their heirs."

Virginia right-of-way had been bought without such a clause, but the cleared grade was now becoming a path for vandals, motorcyclists, and illegal hunters. The steam engine parked at the head of the line in Abingdon was vandalized. Numerous residents argued that N & W was required to return the right-of-way to the original landowners. In December 1977, thirteen landowners signed a petition to that effect and presented it to the Washington County Board of Supervisors. A lawsuit against Norfolk & Western by some of these landowners soon followed.

Norfolk & Western successfully made the case that they owned the rights for right-of-way disposal, and they intended to sell. They further stipulated that they would not sell to a large number of individuals.

In early 1978 the U.S. Forest Service bought the right-of-way between Damascus and Green Cove, a stretch about fourteen miles long, mostly contained in Jefferson National Forest's Mount Rogers National Recreation Area. The Forest Service planned a hiking/biking trail and was strongly supportive of Abingdon's efforts to preserve a longer trail. An additional four miles of right-of-way around Green Cove and Whitetop were purchased by the Forest Service to reach to the North Carolina line, lengthening the trail to eighteen miles. (Peggie Baldwin of Whitetop is currently working to restore the Whitetop Railway Station on Forest Service land. For information write to P.O. Box 81, Whitetop, VA 24292.)

The town of Damascus was soon to receive federal funds through the Virginia Commission for Outdoor Recreation to build a town park. The Town Council was able to use some VCOR funds to buy their three miles of right-of-way to link the town park to the Mount Rogers National Recreation Area.

The trail was now twenty-one miles long. Norfolk & Western was very anxious to sell the remaining thirteen miles of right-of-way—or at least have the bridges and trestles removed—in the summer of 1978. The company's insurance had lapsed since their abandonment of the railway section. If an accident occurred along the corridor, N & W might face serious financial loss. Indeed some local landowners built barricades to stop the movement of people on the right-of-way. The resulting tensions further concerned N & W.

A public hearing held on July 25, 1978, heard some opposition to the trail in addition to vocal and widespread support. Still, the Washington County Board of Supervisors voted down the proposal to purchase the remaining right-of-way. Efforts to get direct help from the Virginia Division of Parks also failed. Meanwhile, French Moore had to contact Norfolk & Western regularly to delay trestle and bridge removal. The Tennessee Valley Authority designated adequate funds for purchasing the right-of-way, but the funds would have to go through the Virginia Division of Parks. The division balked, and nearly two years later the deal still was not complete.

A public hearing in August 1980 showed strong support for the trail, and a group of twelve local residents personally committed about $3,000 each toward the purchase. In the end, private money was not needed. Finally, in September 1981, the Virginia Commission for Outdoor Recreation agreed to allocate $60,000 in federal funds to this project. Combined with TVA funds, the trail's funding was now about $155,000. The towns of Abingdon and Damascus were able to buy the thirteen miles of right-of-way between them. Norfolk & Western was paid a total of $25,000 for the right-of-way on January 4, 1982. The land (103 acres) had an estimated worth of $60,000, so Norfolk & Western was credited with donating $35,000 in the transaction. On February 19, 1982, the town of Abingdon used VCOR funds to pay the Chicago Contracting Company $21,200 for steel bridges along that right-of-way. The wooden trestles were donated by the company. The trail corridor was now thirty-four miles long, half on federal land and half on land owned by local governments.

The trail was incomplete, however, since the bridges and trestles had inadequate floors and no guard rails. The Jacobs Creek Job Corps from Bristol, Tennessee, laid down wooden floors and guard rails on the trestles. Materials for this work included hundreds of pounds of hardware and thousands of feet of treated lumber, costing about $50,000. In 1985 and 1986, members of the U.S. Naval Reserve Constructing Force Supporting Unit No. 1, Detachment Bravo, of Kingsport, Tennessee, gave their time to improve the bridges along the trail.

Even as this work was being done, several landowners opposed the trail. Some were justifiably upset by hunters using the right-of-way as a path to private forestlands to shoot deer. In a few sections, people were driving cars, trucks, and motorcycles on the right-of-way, making the corridor unsafe. Some people living along the trail feared that thieves would use the route.

A major setback came when one of the larger trestles—Number 6, at Mile 4.7, near Watauga—was damaged by a mysterious fire in 1985. Half of the 450-foot structure was destroyed, creating a gap which remained on the nascent trail for more than two years. The cause of the fire was never determined. Even before repairs could be done, however, Congress approved the trail's new designation in March 1986, and the dedication ceremony was held in Damascus in 1987. Finally, with $100,000 from the Virginia Commission for Outdoor Recreation, help from Pittston Coal Company President Gene Mathis, and Jacob's Creek Job Corps workers, the repairs and all handrails and trestle floors were complete in July 1989.

Since 1989, the Virginia Creeper Trail Club, founded by Mel Heiman, has worked constantly as a volunteer organi-

Retired "Virginia Creeper" steam locomotive donated by Norfolk & Western Railway stands under the shelter at the trailhead in Abingdon. (Photo by Michael Pierry, Jr.)

zation to keep the trail clean and safe. Maintenance such as mowing, removal of fallen trees and rocks, and filling eroded sections is done by the towns and the Forest Service. In recent years, volunteers have removed junk from the streams along the trail, and trash cans have been placed at numerous locations.

Deterioration of the thirty-one wooden trestles on the trail is beginning to cause concern within the Forest Service, the Creeper Trail Club, and the towns of Abingdon and Damascus. In 1996 engineers from the Forest Service estimated that about $3 million would be needed for bridge reconstruction work in the next few years. As a safety measure, the trail might eventually close if the trail's trestles are not maintained. You can help by writing your state and national representatives and asking them to help keep the Virginia Creeper Trail healthy.

Forest rangers travel the upper section of the trail on bicycles, looking for illegal activities. Reports of crime along the trail have been uncommon in the last ten years. In 1994, an Emory & Henry College survey of thirty people who own property along the trail found that seventy-five percent were in favor of the trail. This group included many people who said they had opposed the trail when it was first proposed in 1977. Although a few still oppose it, several residents reported that they feel the value of their property has been increased by the presence of the trail.

Ironically, since the late 1980s there has been a revival of local interest in creating a trail on the North Carolina section of the Creeper railroad bed. Unfortunately, recombining all those segments of right-of-way would require 100 percent cooperation from several dozen landowners, some of whom have now built structures on the right-of-way. Recreating a trail route there now would be difficult.

The following people deserve recognition for their work in establishing the National Recreation Trail: Dr. French Moore, Jr.; U.S. Congressman Rick Boucher; Abingdon planner Al Bradley; Bill Fry of Chicago Contracting Company; Abingdon town manager Brent Remsburg; Rob Blackmore of the Virginia Commission for Outdoor Recreation; President R. B. Claytor of Norfolk & Western Railway; Damascus mayor Joseph Rae; President Gene Mathis and Engineer Gerald Borrelli of Pittston Coal Company; Terry Chilcoat, Richard

A Creeper Trail trestle. (Photo by Michael Pierry, Jr.)

Morgan, and Bob Marks of the Tennessee Valley Authority; Tom Taylor of Mount Rogers Planning District; Ted Davis of the Heritage, Conservation and Recreation Service; Joe Brown of the National Park Service; Fred Walker and Ben

Bolen of the Virginia Department of Conservation and Economic Development; Martin Hassinger of Hassinger Lumber Company; Earl Coalson; W. D. Young; Dr. David Brilhart; Howard Kelley; Bill Cole; Walter Hendricks; and Dr. Mel Heiman.

These organizations provided support in the trail's creation: U.S. Forest Service; town of Abingdon; town of Damascus; Virginia Commission for Outdoor Recreation (within the Virginia Division of Parks); Tennessee Valley Authority; Norfolk & Western Railway; The Heritage, Conservation and Recreation Service (within the Department of the Interior); Jacobs Creek Job Corps in Bristol, Tennessee; Flatwoods Job Corps in Coeburn, Virginia; Naval Reserve Constructing Force in Kingsport, Tennessee; Bristol Steel Company; and Pittston Coal Company.

Floods were common and the bridges were often destroyed. Perhaps the worst flood was in 1916: this shows rail cars and debris in Whitetop Laurel Creek near Creek Junction that year. (Photo courtesy of Martin Hassinger.)

CREEPER TIMELINE:
RAILWAY AND TRAIL

1887 Founding of Abingdon Coal & Iron Railroad—no tracks laid

1889 Wilton E. Mingea, a freight agent for N & W, buys all assets. Company is renamed "Virginia-Carolina Railway." Town of Damascus is laid out in hopes of an iron & steel industry.

1899 Mingea grades and lays track, Abingdon to Damascus

1900 Feb 7: First train runs from Abingdon to Damascus, 16.2 miles

1905 V-C RR records profit of $32,000; RR is extended from Damascus to Taylors Valley

1906 Konnarock founded by Hassinger Lumber Co.

1907 New Virginia, Carolina & Southern RR built from Taylors Valley to Creek Junction

1908 VC & S RR extended to Konnarock

1909 V-C RR records profit of $36,000

1911 Norfolk & Western begins financing V-C RR

1912 V-C RR records profit of $8,000. N & W purchases 51% of assets from Mingea. RR is extended from Creek Junction to Whitetop Station. V-C RR purchases Hassinger's RR link to Konnarock

1914 July: V-C RR completed to Elkland, N.C.

1915 Daily traffic: 6 freights, and 2 passenger trains

1916 June: N & W purchases remaining V-C RR stock interests; July: Flood causes severe damage

1917 Forest fire causes severe damage

1919 August 19: V-C RR becomes "Abingdon Branch" of N & W RR; N & W pays $2 million for 76 miles of track, land & buildings; George P. Johnson replaces Wilton Mingea as president

1924 Daily traffic drops to 3 freights, 2 passenger trains

1928 December 24: Hassinger Lumber Company closes in Konnarock

1929 Daily traffic: 2 freights, 1 passenger train

1930 Flood causes severe damage: no trains run for 6 months; Branch to Konnarock is abandoned

1933 Eleanor Roosevelt visits Whitetop for Music Festival
1935 Stone for Blue Ridge Parkway moves on Abingdon Branch
1940 Flood causes severe damage, repairs cost $167,000
1942 Legendary train rescue of snowbound critically ill pregnant woman
1954 Daily traffic: 1 mixed (freight/passenger) train
1956 August 9: O. W. Link takes famous photo at Green Cove Station
1957 Steam engines are replaced by diesel; July: Photos by Link make national press
1962 May 20: Last passenger train runs
1968 Weekly traffic: 2 freight trains
1971 N & W begins seeking approval to close Abingdon Branch
1974 Weekly traffic: 1 freight train
1976 July 30: N & W Railway gets approval to close Abingdon Branch
1977 March 31: Last train runs on the track; Chicago company agrees to pay $402,000 for track as scrap; right-of-way in North Carolina reverts to landowners
1978 US Forest Service buys right-of-way between Damascus & NC line
1982 March: Towns of Abingdon & Damascus buy rest of right-of-way for $28,000
1985 Fire damages trestle #6 near Watauga
1986 Congress designates right-of-way as National Recreation Trail
1987 June: Dedicated as National Recreation Trail
1989 July: Repairs and construction of handrails and floorboards complete
1997 Annual traffic: 25,000 people on foot, bike, and horse

CHAPTER THREE: TRAIL FEATURES

Mileages are according to mile markers set along the trail, beginning from the trailhead in Abingdon and ending at the North Carolina state line (34.3). The original cement markers (most now 80 years old) were positioned in reference to the Abingdon train station, about one half mile away from the trailhead. Around Damascus and Taylors Valley, some of those old markers are missing. New markers for Miles 1 through 7 have been placed by volunteers, including the local Boy Scouts. These new markers indicate actual trail distance (mileage from the trailhead). Please note that all the rest indicate about a half mile more distance than the truth. For example, Mile Marker 11.0 is about 10.5 miles from the trailhead.

Mile 0 to 1 Cherry Lane

0.0 parking lot; old steam engine; trestle 250 feet long; elevation: 2,040 ft. 0% grade next mile

0.1 parking lot for larger vehicles; giant white oak tree; bench

0.2 bench

0.3 park with benches and tables—once a turnaround for engines

0.5 view of large farm

0.7 bench

0.8 Interstate 81, this section opened in 1960s

Mile 1 to 2

1.0 Mile Marker; elevation: 2,040 ft. -1.1% grade next mile

1.1 Winterham Estates

1.7 edge of ancient shale rock formation

1.8 shaded cove south of trail

Mile 2 to 3 through the Great Knobs

2.0 Mile Marker; elevation: 1,980 ft. -0.8% grade next mile

2.1 great views of deep forest
2.2 site of old farmstead in hollow
2.9 curved trestle over Dry Branch 340 feet long

Mile 3 to 4

3.0 Mile Marker; elevation: 1,940 ft. -0.4% grade next mile
3.1 trestle over Berry Creek 230 feet long
3.3 edge of ancient shale rock formation
3.5 metal "3.5" Mile Marker on tree
3.6 nice view of pasture
3.7 bridge over Fifteen Mile Creek 480 feet long; gate
3.8 parking lot; Route 677 crossing (poor visibility—use caution); gate
3.9 site of old Watauga Station & siding, removed 1934

Mile 4 to 5

4.0 Mile Marker; elevation: 1,920 ft. -0.4% grade next mile
4.1 railbed in long cut
4.2 many yellow poplars
4.3 rose bushes
4.4 redcedar grove with view of old barn
4.5 bridge 320 feet long; great views

Mile 5 to 6 great views in the River Knobs

(*NOTE: Original cement markers from here to Whitetop are one half mile closer to Abingdon than they indicate.*)

5.0 Mile Marker; elevation: 1,900 ft. -0.8% grade next mile
5.3 trestle 450 feet long; great view to the west
5.4 large rock face
5.6 shaded cove with old-growth forest; great view down to river
5.7 old telegraph poles
5.8 great view down to river
5.9 narrow cut through shale rock

Mile 6 to 7 mostly through Smith Farm pasture

6.0 Mile Marker; elevation: 1,860 ft. -1.1% grade next mile; large old oak
6.1 nice view east to Iron Mountain
6.2 trail through pasture of Smith Farm
6.3 curved trestle 550 feet long
6.4 many limestone rocks

6.5 sinkhole
6.6 bridge 300 feet long; great view of river and across pasture
6.9 cattle gate

Mile 7 to 8 over South Holston Lake

7.0 Mile Marker; elevation: 1,800 ft. -0.6% grade next mile
7.1 railbed cut through limestone
7.2 cliff 30 feet high; rock bench; large old oak; loud rapids
7.4 bridge 100 feet long
7.7 old telegraph poles
7.8 rock benches; South Holston Lake trestle: 529 feet long; elevation of railbed:1,770 feet
7.9 cattle gate

Mile 8 to 9 through pasture

8.0 original Mile Marker; elevation: 1,770 ft. -0.4% grade next mile
8.1 large old tree; nice views
8.2 cliff; quiet river
8.3 cattle gate
8.4 sinkhole pasture
8.5 groundhog burrow; blackberry bushes; large cherry tree
8.7 cattle gate; large sycamore tree
8.8 large, noisy rapids can be heard
8.9 40-foot cliff; cattle gate

Mile 9 to 10 through Alvarado

9.0 original Mile Marker; elevation: 1,750 ft. +0.4% grade next mile; parking lot; lowest point on trail
9.1 Alvarado; old "Alvarado Grocery"/post office retired in 1956
9.2 loud rapids
9.3 intersection of Routes 710 & 711; 1820 farmhouse
9.4 rapids; nice view across South Fork Holston River
9.5 cliff 40 feet high; deep quiet river
9.6 rapids; bridge over Route 711 and Rockhouse Run
9.7 farm with old log structure and root cellar
9.8 view across quiet river to cliffs 50 feet high
9.9 large rocks; small parking lot beside Route 711; road crossing

Mile 10 to 11 rock walls, farms, and cliffs

10.0 original Mile Marker; elevation: 1,770 ft. +0.6% grade next mile

10.1 loud rapids

10.2 view of rock cliffs

10.3 nice view along trail; large sycamore trees

10.4 gate; nice view across river rock wall

10.5 nice view of farmhouse

10.6 rock wall; view of rock cliffs

10.7 rock wall

10.8 loud rapids

10.9 bridge over Gimlet Branch; rock bench; parking lot; Route 712 crossing; old steel bridge

Mile 11 to 12

11.0 original Mile Marker; elevation: 1,800 ft. 0% grade next mile; Delmar; site of old station

11.0 Canada goose nest close to houses

11.1 old root cellar

11.3 rock cliff; shady section; nice view of dogwoods

11.4 nice view of river

11.6 apple tree; large pasture

11.7 rock wall; large pasture; trail rough here

11.8 view of long rock wall with cherry trees; large pasture

11.9 view of rock wall

Mile 12 to 13

12.0 original Mile Marker; missing elevation: 1,800 ft. +0.6% grade next mile

12.1 great view across river; sinkhole

12.2 rapids; long shady section begins; rocks

12.3 quiet river but you can hear traffic on US 58 across river

12.4 great view across river to rock wall

12.5 loud rapids; narrow cut in rock

12.6 Drowning Ford; site of old siding; US 58 passes overhead; access to US 58 on Route 711

12.7 view of cliffs across river; limits of town of Damascus; water gauge towers and gondola

12.8 view of high cliffs across river; Damascus water treat-

Quiet waters of Whitetop Laurel Creek. These cobbles and boulders will become hiding places for trout in the deeper, faster spring flow. (Photo by Edward H. Davis.)

ment plant
12.9 solid waste disposal facility

Mile 13 to 14

13.0 original Mile Marker; elevation: 1,830 ft. +1.1% grade next mile; rapids; great view to mountains
13.1 access to US 58
13.2 houses made of round river stones
13.5 view of high cliff across river
13.6 telegraph pole; rapids
13.7 Trails Restaurant across US 58 (breakfast 6:30 to 10:00 a.m.); old limestone foundation
13.8 light display every Christmas
13.9 Conoco station across US 58

Mile 14 to 15

14.0 original Mile Marker missing; elevation: 1,860 ft. +0.4% grade next mile; site of old schoolhouse
14.1 nice view of barn
14.2 site of rechanneled river; track was rerouted here in 1958
14.3 site of old siding
14.5 only place where original tracks remain, partially buried
14.7 Columbus McKinnon plant (was Vail's Mill)
14.8 nice view of cliffs across river
14.9 nice view west to mountains

Mile 15 to 16 old industrial landscape

15.0 original Mile Marker; elevation: 1,880 ft. +0.6% grade next mile; rapids
15.1 large rocks; site of old siding
15.2 old furniture factory; old mill race
15.4 old dam; large lumber yard
15.5 rapids; view of rock wall across river
15.6 view of stone silo; shady stretch
15.8 site of large water tank 1924-53

Mile 16 to 17 through the Town of Damascus

16.0 original Mile Marker; elevation: 1,910 ft. +0.9% grade next mile; parking lot; town park; Appalachian Trail
16.1 Blue Blaze shuttle service is 3 blocks north; site of old

depot and siding

16.2 Minute-ette Food Market; Quincey's Pizza is ½ block north; site of old 60-ft. turntable for engines, retired 1936

16.4 trestle over Laurel Creek 540 feet long

16.5 site of old siding

16.8 end Damascus, begin US Forest Service property

Mile 17 to 18

17.0 original Mile Marker missing; elevation: 1,960 ft. +0.9% grade next mile

17.1 Appalachian Trail turns off across US 58 and uphill

17.4 crossing Route 91 (use caution)

17.5 rapids

17.6 parking lot on US 58 uphill from trail; sunny section with kudzu; large yellow poplar

17.8 power line crossing; site of old narrow-gauge track crossing; site of old sand storage building, retired 1934

17.9 Laureldale; site of old depot and siding, retired 1934

Mile 18 to 19

18.0 original Mile Marker; missing elevation: 2,010 ft. +1.3% grade next mile

18.1 lots of kudzu

18.2 quiet creek

18.3 gate, old parking lot (now closed)

18.4 steel bridge 90 feet long

18.5 large red oak, earleaf magnolia, white oak

18.6 bridge 100 feet long

18.7 large white oaks; bridge 120 feet long; striped maple; large red oak & hemlock

18.8 rapids; lots of rhododendron

18.9 shady cove with large yellow poplar and rhododendron; very shady section

Mile 19 to 20

19.0 original Mile Marker (hard to see); elevation: 2,080 ft. +1.8% grade next mile

19.1 small white pine grove; traffic on US 58 can be heard

19.2 cliff rhododendron

Forests are maturing today along the trail. Professor George Treadwell stands at the base of a large tuliptree at about Mile 21.0. (Photo by Edward H. Davis.)

19.3 striped maple hemlock
19.4 large white pine grove begins
19.6 ruins of old house across Whitetop Laurel Creek
19.7 white pine grove ends
19.8 rapids; cliff bridge; cables protect against flood; rocks show drill holes from 1906
19.9 side path north through white pines to US 58

Mile 20 to 21

20.0 original Mile Marker (hard to see); elevation: 2,180 ft. +0.9% grade next mile; large hemlock
20.1 cliff; large yellow poplar
20.2 Forest Service campsite in white pine grove; path to Whitetop Laurel Creek
20.3 old telegraph poles
20.4 parking lot; large yellow poplars; large red oak
20.6 US 58 passes close to trail

Mile 21 to 22 numerous large yellow poplars

21.0 original Mile Marker; elevation: 2,230 ft. +1.7% grade next mile; bridge

Mile 22 to 23 nice views of creek & forest

22.0 Mile Marker elevation: 2,320 ft. +1.3% grade next mile
22.1 bridge 90 feet long
22.6 access trail to Appalachian Trail
22.7 enter Taylors Valley
22.9 parking lot; old crew car with public rest rooms

Mile 23 to 24 Taylors Valley

23.0 original Mile Marker missing; elevation: 2,390 ft. +1.5% grade next mile; site of old station
23.1 view north to Straight Mountain; close to private homes
23.2 curved bridge 164 feet long; large white oak
23.3 view to open field
23.6 fields and homes
23.7 fields and homes

Mile 24 to 25

24.0 original Mile Marker; elevation: 2,470 ft. +1.1% grade next mile; bridge 120 feet long

Mile 25 to 26

25.0 original Mile Marker; elevation: 2,530 ft. +1.3% grade

Unknown man poses circa 1910 with a giant tree, now gone, on Whitetop Mountain. (Photo courtesy of Martin Hassinger.)

next mile

Mile 26 to 27

26.0 original Mile Marker (hidden in leaves); elevation: 2,600 ft. +2.3% grade next mile

Mile 27 to 28 Creek Junction

27.0 original Mile Marker; elevation: 2,720 ft. +2.3% grade next mile

27.2 Hassinger monument at confluence of Whitetop and Green Cove creeks; trestle 563 feet long

27.3 bridge 200 feet long

27.4 rapids

27.5 unusually large striped maple (4" diam.)

27.6 fire cherry

27.7 Fraser magnolia; nice view along trail

27.8 many yellow poplars and eastern hemlocks

27.9 Fraser magnolia

Mile 28 to 29

28.0 original Mile Marker; elevation: 2,840 ft. +2.7% grade next mile; small bridge; nice view of stream

28.1 large yellow poplars

28.2 large hemlocks

28.3 gate (use caution); small bridge

28.4 sunny section

28.6 hemlock and rhododendron

28.7 large basswood; small bridge

28.8 large red maple

28.9 beaver dam; swamp; nice view of pasture

Mile 29 to 30 homes, apple trees, and blackberry bushes

29.0 original Mile Marker; elevation: 2,980 ft. +2.5% grade next mile; fire cherry tree

29.1 old barn; blackberries; access to Rt. 726

29.2 mountain laurel and yellow poplar

29.5 gate; Fraser magnolia

29.6 large ash; road crossing Rt. 726 (one mile from US 58)

29.7 large rocks; hemlocks

29.8 short bridge; blackberries

29.9 access to Rt. 600

Mile 30 to 31 among the barns and homes of Green Cove

30.0 original Mile Marker missing; elevation: 3,110 ft. +2.1% grade next mile

30.1 large oak

30.7 restored Green Cove station; public toilets

30.8 nice view of Beech Mountain and Green Cove

30.9 road crossing; large red maple; trail becomes steeper toward Whitetop

Mile 31 to 32 many yellow poplars

31.0 original Mile Marker; elevation: 3,220 ft. +2.8% grade next mile

31.1 gate; view through opening in forest

31.2 large yellow poplar

31.3 very large black locust; flame azalea

31.4 large hemlocks

31.6 nice view over valley

31.7 shaded cove

31.8 Grayson-Washington county line, fire cherry

31.9 striped maple

Mile 32 to 33

32.0 original Mile Marker; elevation: 3,370 ft. +2.9% grade next mile; only 600 feet from Tennessee line

32.1 shaded cove with large yellow poplars

32.2 large red maple; striped maple

32.3 views of ice and wind damage caused in early 1993

32.5 large yellow poplar

32.6 flame azalea

32.7 high trestle 283 feet long, 66 feet above High Trestle Branch

32.9 large white oak

Mile 33 to 34

33.0 original Mile Marker; elevation: 3,525 ft. +3.2% grade to Whitetop Christmas tree farm; large white oak

33.3 enter Whitetop community; elevation 3,576 ft. (Tennessee Divide), highest point on trail; parking; view of cemetery; site of old Whitetop station

Mile 34 to 34.3

34.0 original Mile Marker; elevation: 3,500 ft.

34.3 Virginia-North Carolina line; end of trail

The restored Green Cove Station is at Mile 31.0. (Photo by Edward H. Davis.)

The narrow-gauge engine on display in Damascus at Mile 16.0 was once used to haul logs. (Photo by Edward H. Davis.)

CHAPTER FOUR: RESOURCES

AMERICAN CHESTNUT FOUNDATION'S MEADOWVIEW RESEARCH FARMS

In 1989, these research facilities were begun in an effort to rejuvenate the American chestnut tree in Southern Appalachia. Under the guidance of plant pathologist Dr. Fred Hebard, more than 7,000 trees have been planted on more than one hundred acres. American chestnut trees are cross-bred with naturally resistant Chinese chestnut trees, until they are "mostly" American while still carrying the blight-resistant genes of the full Chinese variety. When they are $^{15}/_{16}$ American and also resistant in about ten years, the organization will distribute nuts to the public for planting. To visit the research farm, take exit 24 off Interstate 81, turn southeast, and go 0.3 miles. The main facility is on the left.

Dr. Fred Hebard
Meadowview Research Farms
Meadowview, VA 24361
540-944-4631

MIDDLE FORK HOLSTON WATER QUALITY COMMITTEE

If you want to help promote better land use practices in this or any other watershed nearby, you may want to see the work of this local organization. The MFHWQC has been working on water quality here for almost fifteen years. The most convenient office follows:

Natural Resources Conservation Service Field Office
160 Cummings St.
Abingdon, VA 24210-3202
540-628-8187

The Creek Junction area along the trail is now part of the Mount Rogers National Recreation Area. Nearby at Mile 27.0 is a plaque commemorating the Hassinger Lumber Company. (Photo by Edward H. Davis.)

MOUNT ROGERS NATIONAL RECREATION AREA

Most of the trail between Damascus and Whitetop Station is within the bounds of the Mount Rogers National Recreation Area. This federally protected land was established by Congress in 1966 as a unit of the Jefferson National Forest. It contains 115,000 acres of forested mountains, streams, and open land managed for recreation, conservation, and timber. Within the recreation area are several wilderness areas set aside for hiking and camping. Maps to these wilderness areas can be obtained at the Visitor's Center.

The beautiful Visitor's Center is located at the headquarters about seven miles south of Marion (take exit 45 off I-81), just off Virginia Rt. 15. Here visitors can learn about the 400 miles of trails and six established campgrounds in the recreation area, see exhibits about the area's nature and history, enjoy an acclaimed short film about the area, and talk to forest rangers. There is also a shop with books, maps, T-shirts, and supplies. During the summer, the Visitor's Center is open seven days a week.

Mount Rogers National Recreation Area Headquarters
Rt. 1 Box 303
Marion, VA 24354
540-783-5196

THE APPALACHIAN TRAIL

The Appalachian Trail coincides with the Creeper Trail in two stretches: just uphill from Damascus (Mile 16.5 to Mile 16.9) and at Creek Junction (Mile 26.4 to Mile 27.2). Between these two points the trails also run closely parallel to a feeder trail (marked "TO A.T.") just downhill from Taylors Valley at Mile 22.6.

The Appalachian Trail was first conceived in 1921 by Benton McKaye, a hiker and regional planner. Thousands of volunteers worked together to purchase land, clear paths, and build bridges and shelters; and on August 14, 1937, the trail became a reality. Now it runs from Maine to Georgia as a National Scenic Trail more than 2,150 miles long, crossing eight national forests. Virginia contains the longest portion (541 miles). In 1968 the United States Congress authorized protection of the A.T. from development encroaching along the narrow path. This allowed purchase of easements and land along many beautiful stretches of the Appalachians so that the trail will always pass mostly through peaceful forest scenery.

The A.T. is maintained through the steady work of local clubs. It is cleaned, maintained, and protected by about 4,000 volunteers organized into thirty-one chapters of the Appalachian Trail Conference. To join fellow hikers in preserving this natural resource, contact the following organizations:

Mount Rogers Appalachian Trail Club
Rt. 7 Box 345
Abingdon, VA 24210
540-628-2601

Appalachian Trail Conference
P.O. Box 807
Harpers Ferry, WV 25425
304-535-6331

Mount Rogers Outfitters
546 Laurel Avenue
Damascus, VA 24236
540-475-5416

RAILS-TO-TRAILS CONSERVANCY

The Virginia Creeper Trail was one of the country's first rail-to-trail conversions, of which there have been about 700 since 1975. The organization which supports conversions of abandoned railroad corridors is the Rails-to-Trails Conservancy. Some other trails nearby are the New River Trail and the Washington & Old Dominion Railroad Regional Park in Virginia, the Greenbrier River Trail in West Virginia, and the Baltimore & Annapolis Trail in Maryland. For a directory of all rail trails in the U.S. call 1-800-888-7747.

For more information contact:

Rails-to-Trails Conservancy
1400 Sixteenth St., NW Suite 300
Washington, DC 20036
202-797-5400

THE VIRGINIA CREEPER TRAIL CLUB

The Virginia Creeper Trail Club is an incorporated non-profit organization, purposing "to plan, promote, coordinate and execute programs designed to educate and stimulate the awareness of the general public concerning various aspects of the natural environment of the western portion of Virginia and the flora and fauna thereof, and to help develop, maintain and provide public access to conduct public education programs regarding the scenic and natural qualities of a por-

The Creeper Trail is used all year by cyclists, walkers, joggers, and horseback riders. This trestle is just east of Watauga at Mile 5.0. (Photo by Edward H. Davis.)

tion of a right-of-way formerly owned by Norfolk & Western Railway between the Town of Abingdon and the Town of Damascus, and/or that right-of-way more commonly known as the Virginia Creeper Trail extending from Abingdon to Whitetop Station." (By-laws of the Virginia Creeper Trail Club, Ltd.)

The club sponsors regular events on the trail, including Fall Fun Day and Clean Up Day. The club has also worked to install benches, self-closing gates, Mile Markers, and safety reflectors as well as making other repairs and improvements on the trail. The club cooperates with the National Forest Service in caring for the upper section of the trail, which is on U.S.F.S. property, and with the towns of Abingdon and Damascus, owners of the lower section of the trail.

There are several meetings a year, including the annual meeting at which officers are elected. Anyone can be a member simply by signing up and paying the annual dues ($10 in 1997). Meetings are usually held at the Washington County Library at the intersection of Valley and Oak Hill streets in Abingdon. For information write:

Virginia Creeper Trail Club
P.O. Box 2382
Abingdon, VA 24212-2382

BLUE BLAZE SHUTTLE SERVICE

Based on Laurel Avenue in Damascus (the trail's midpoint), Blue Blaze Shuttle Service has been in operation since 1991. For a fee, shuttle service is provided for hikers, bicyclists, and their gear to the trailheads of the Virginia Creeper Trail, Appalachian Trail, and Iron Mountain Trail. A large fleet of mountain bikes is available to rent. A helmet and water bottle are provided for each bike rented. No small children's bikes are available.

The most common shuttle arrangements are to park in Damascus and be carried to Whitetop Mountain for the ride downhill. Some arrange to park at Whitetop or Abingdon and be carried in the opposite direction. Between mid-April and late October, one can reserve a seat on the shuttle bus leaving Damascus each Saturday and Sunday at 9:30, 11:00, 12:30, and 2:00, and leaving Abingdon at 9:00 and 10:30. During weekdays and in the off-season, a variety of arrangements can be made; but don't forget that all shuttle service is by reservation and otherwise first come, first served. During peak periods (the first warm weekend of spring, nice days in the summer, and autumn-leaf-viewing times) reservations fill up quickly. Try to make reservations at least two weeks in advance.

This shuttle service is especially popular with large groups. In recent years cyclists have arranged several "moonlight rides" when the night sky is clear and the moon is full. If interested, contact Blue Blaze. Headlights are needed and only experienced cyclists are allowed.

Blue Blaze Shuttle Service
227 West Laurel Avenue
Damascus, VA 24236
540-475-5095

VIRGINIA TRAFFIC LAWS FOR CYCLISTS

When riding a bike on roads near the Creeper Trail, remember to obey all Virginia vehicle laws:

Traffic regulations: You must obey all traffic signs, signals, markings, and lights.

Required equipment: Bicycles ridden on the highway must have brakes that skid the wheels on clean, dry pavement. Bicycles ridden between sunset and sunrise must have a white light visible 500 feet to the front and a red reflector on the rear visible 300 feet to the rear. A red light visible 500 feet to the rear may be used in place of or in addition to the red reflector.

Where to ride: You must ride with the flow of traffic. You must ride as close as practical to the right hand curb or edge. Exceptions are when overtaking and passing another vehicle;

when preparing for a left turn; when people, animals, parked cars, or other objects make traveling unsafe; and when narrow lane widths do not provide sufficient room for a motor vehicle or bicycle to share the lane. Ride in single file on highways; riding two or more abreast is permitted on paths. Ride on sidewalks only if not prohibited by local ordinance. On sidewalks, pedestrians always have the right of way. You must sound a horn or bell before passing a pedestrian. You have the right of way on sidewalks when a motorist pulls out of a driveway.

Changing directions: You must signal your intention to turn, stop, or change direction.

For your safety: You must keep at least one hand on the handlebars at all times. Hitching rides on moving vehicles is against the law.

If you have an accident: You must report to the police any accident that involves death, injury, or property damage. You must give your name and address to any persons involved in the accident. If the accident involves damage to an unattended vehicle or other property, you must make a reasonable effort to find the owner and report the accident. If the owner cannot be located, you must leave a note at the accident site and report the accident to the police within twenty-four hours. For more information contact:

Public Information Office
Virginia Department of Motor Vehicles
P.O. Box 27412
Richmond, VA 23269
804-367-0041

BIBLIOGRAPHY

"Backtracking into our History." *Virginia Wildlife*, V.50, n.1 (January 1989).

Bartlett, Charles S., Jr. and Thomas H. Biggs. *Geology of the Abingdon, Wyndale, Holston Valley and Shady Valley Quadrangles*. Richmond: Commonwealth of Virginia Department of Conservation and Development, 1980.

Berry, Wendell. "The Wild Geese," in *The Country of Marriage*. San Diego: Harvest/HBJ, 1973, p. 24.

Cochran, Bill. "Elk Stocking Idea Gets a 'Maybe'." *The Roanoke Times*, 17 February, 1997, 36.

Blanton, Bill. "Walking the Line." *The Plow*, 1 November, 1977, 11-20.

Dietrich, R. V. *Geology and Virginia*. Charlottesville: University of Virginia, 1970.

Frye, Keith. *Roadside Geology of Virginia*. Missoula, Montana: Mountain Press, 1986.

Gooch, Edwin O. *Iron in Virginia*. Richmond: Commonwealth of Virginia Department of Conservation and Development, 1954.

Hampton, Tom and John Jessee. "Region III." Virginia Department of Game and Inland Fisheries, *Virginia Freshwater Fishing Guide*, 1996 edition. Richmond: Commonwealth of Virginia, 1996.

Harrison, Hal. *Wood Warbler's World.* New York: Simon & Schuster, 1984.

Hassinger, Luther C. "The Lumber Industry in Southwest Virginia." *Washington County Historical Society Bulletin* (Spring 1964), 5-16.

Hicks, Mike. "A History of the Abingdon Branch Line." Unpublished paper on file at Norfolk & Western Railway offices in Roanoke, no date.

Hunt, Charles B. *Physiography of the United States.* San Francisco: W. H. Freeman, 1967.

Jones, Robert S. "Days of Iron and Steam: Recollections of the Abingdon-West Jefferson Line." *The Plow.* May 1976, 13, 16.

Jurney, R. C. *Soil Survey, Washington County, Virginia* (Principle Soil Scientist: J. W. Moon). Washington, D.C.: U.S. Department of Agriculture, 1945.

Kirk, Donald. "The Call of the Coyote: Yes, You Can Hear It in the Blue Ridge." *Blue Ridge Country.* 3, 5 (September-October 1990), 36-37.

Koester, Tony. "Reflections on the Abingdon Branch." *Railroad Model Craftsman.* (September 1975), 44-51.

Lewis, Lloyd D. "An Abingdon Branch Accolade" *Trains*, 44, 8 (June 1984), 21-28.

Link, O. Winston. "The Mixed Train." *Trains* (July 1957): 31-43.

Little, Elbert. *National Audubon Society Field Guide to North American Trees—Eastern Region.* New York: Alfred Knopf, 1980.

McDaniel, Lynda, "How to Read a Wildflower," *North Carolina Wildlife* April 1996: 15-19.

McKenna, George. "Elk in Virginia." *Virginia Wildlife* (October, 1962), p.6.

McKibben, Bill. "An Explosion of Green." *The Atlantic Monthly* (April 1995), 61-83.

Mohn, Larry. "Virginia Trout Guide." Virginia Department of Game and Inland Fisheries, *Virginia Freshwater Fishing Guide*, 1996 edition. Richmond: Commonwealth of Virginia, 1996.

Mongle, John. "Funds Ok'd for Creeper Conversion." Bristol *Herald Courier*, August 30, 1978.

Mongle, John. "New Push to Begin for Area Hike Trail." Bristol *Herald Courier*, April 7, 1978.

Mongle, John. "TVA to Acquire Part of Old Railway Line." Bristol *Herald Courier*, June 12, 1978.

Moore, Jr., French. "From Rails to Trails." *Mountain Times*, 7,1 (Spring 1992), 21.

Mount Rogers Planning District Commission. *Recreation Resources, Mount Rogers District: An Analysis and Plan for Development*. Marion, Virginia: Mount Rogers Planning District Commission, 1970.

Niering, William and Nancy Olmstead. *The Audubon Society Field Guide to North American Wildflowers, Eastern Edition*. New York: Alfred A. Knopf, 1979.

"No Timber Reserve but Lumber Mills." *Damascus Blade*, 3 March 1907.

Ogle, Douglas. "The Highest Mountains in Virginia: Mount Rogers and Whitetop or Balsam and Meadow Mountains?" *Virginia Minerals*, 41,4 (November 1995), 25-32.

Peattie, Donald C. *A Natural History of Trees of Eastern and Central North America.* Boston: Houghton Mifflin, 1966.

Peterson, Lee Allen. *Edible Wild Plants.* Peterson Field Guide Series No. 23. Boston: Houghton Mifflin, 1977.

Petrides, George. *A Field Guide to Eastern Trees.* Peterson Field Guide Series, No. 11. Boston: Houghton Mifflin, 1988.

Rails-to-Trails Conservancy. *Secrets of Successful Rail Trails.* Washington, DC: Rails-to-trails Conservancy, 1993.

Rankin, Douglas W. "Stratigraphy and Structure of Precambrian Rocks in Northwestern North Carolina." *Studies of Appalachian Geology: Central and Southern.* Eds. George W. Fisher, F. J. Pettijohn, J. C. Reed, Jr., and Kenneth N. Weaver. New York: Interscience, 1970.

Rankin, Douglas W. The Volcanogenic Mount Rogers Formation and the Overlying Glaciogenic Konnarock Formation: Two Late Protozoic Units in Southwestern Virginia. (U.S. Geological Survey Bulletin No. 2029.) Washington, D.C.: Department of the Interior, 1993.

Schweibert, Ernest. *Trout.* Vol. 1. New York: E. P. Dutton, 1978.

Striplin, E. F. P. *The Norfolk & Western: A History.* Roanoke: Norfolk & Western Railway, 1981.

Stupka, Arthur. *Wildflowers in Color.* New York: Harper Colophon, 1982.

Sturgill, Mack H. “Mount Rogers Named for Founder of M.I.T.” *Washington County News*. 25 March 1992.

Tee-Van, Helen Damrosch. *Small Mammals*. New York: Alfred A. Knopf, 1966.

Thomas, Vaughn, ed. *Appalachian Trail Guide to Southwest Virginia*. Harpers Ferry, West Virginia: Appalachian Trail Conference, 1994.

U.S. Commission on Fish and Fisheries. “Report of Operations at the Wytheville Station, Virginia, January 1 1885 to June 30, 1887.” in Report of the Commissioner, Part XIV. Washington, D.C.: Government Printing Office, 1889.

U.S. Forest Service. “Incomplete Working Paper for Analysis of the Management Situation for the Jefferson National Forest.” August 1996.

U.S. Geological Survey. 7 1/2 Minute Quadrangle Maps: Abingdon, VA; Damascus, VA; Konnarock, VA; Laurel Bloomery, TN-VA; Park, NC-TN-VA. Washington, D.C.: Department of the Interior, various dates.

Villani, John. *100 Best Small Art Towns in America*. San Francisco: John Muir, 1996.

Virginia Department of Game and Inland Fisheries. *Freshwater and Saltwater Fishing Regulations 1996*. Richmond: Commonwealth of Virginia, 1996.

Virginia Department of Game and Inland Fisheries. *Hunting and Trapping Regulations, 1996-97*. Richmond: Commonwealth of Virginia, 1996.

Virginia Society of Ornithologists. *Birds of Virginia Checklist*. Lynchburg: Virginia Society of Ornithologists, no date.

Virginia-Carolina Railway. Unpublished Right-of-way and Track Map. Abingdon, Virginia: Virginia-Carolina Railway Office of the Engineer, 1914.

Wilson, Carolyn. "Green Cove Station Being Renovated." *Bristol Herald Courier*, 22 August 1991.

Woodward, Susan. "The Five Physiographic Provinces of Virginia." *Virginia Explorer*, 10, 1 (Winter 1994), 2-9.

By joining the Virginia Creeper Trail Club, you may help preserve its beauty. (Photo by Edward H. Davis.)